Dear Geoff,

TELL THEM THAT I AM ALIVE

May the Lord Jesus Christ bless
you and keep you,

Brian Hallwell

i

TELL THEM THAT I AM ALIVE

Brian A Halliwell

<Brian Halliwell>

<2016>

First Printing: 2016

ISBN-13:978-1539779193

ISBN-10:153977919X

Email: brian@brianhalliwell.com
Website: www.brianhalliwell.com

Cover illustration is a photograph of sunrise over Swansea Bay taken by Brian Halliwell. Please see page 160/161 to understand the significance of this photo to Brian.

In loving memory of Stella Halliwell 1938 - 2014

Contents

Foreword

Recommendation and Endorsement.

I first met Brian Halliwell in 2013 when I spoke at a Pastors' Gathering in Swansea to introduce the Bible College of Wales to them. I remember after the meeting, Brian came up to me and gave me a prophetic word that involved bringing the memorial stone on a plinth which once occupied a prominent place in front of the Derwen Fawr House back to its original position. The previous management had relocated it to a nice shady but less significant area in front of the Bake House. It was at the dedication of Derwen Fawr in 1931, as a testament and a witness to God's faithfulness and providence, that Mr. Rees Howells had placed on a stone plinth at the front of the house a simple oval stone which had written on one side "Jehovah Jireh" and on the other side "Faith is Substance". I felt the fear of God in my heart.

So when the construction of the Derwen Fawr facility began, we gave instructions to our contractors to bring back the plinth to its original position and on the day that this was done, something significant shifted in the unseen realm. That was the first step in many we would take to restore spiritually the legacy of Mr Rees Howells.

That was my first impression of Brian. He is a man who hears the voice of God and fears God. Over the next few years, I would get to experience this first-hand. Over and over again, he would send me prophetic words that God would give to him whilst praying, usually early in the morning. I took all those prophecies seriously, and prayed through each one of them. It is not unusual to have Brian stand up in church to give a prophetic utterance like the prophets of old. His loud booming voice would break forth and thunder in our hearts. Yes, Brian is a prophet and a man who fears God.

In this book, he chronicles carefully and with intricate detail his life with Stella, his beloved wife and his experiences here at the Bible College. I would recommend this book because Brian has lived the life and paid the price as well. He serves as an advisor to the Directors of the Bible College of Wales.

Rev Yang Tuck Yoong
Senior Pastor
Cornerstone Community Church, Singapore .
Director
Bible College of Wales

Writer's Introduction

I had the privilege of meeting Brian Halliwell during 2013 when my wife and I began attending the Tuesday morning worship and prayer times focusing on revival at the Bible College of Wales. We live some 40 miles distant from Swansea and sadly we never had the privilege of meeting Stella (who by this time was in hospital) but I would often chat to Brian at the meetings. My wife and I attended Stella's funeral at the College in June 2014 – a truly amazing celebration of a life devoted to her Lord - and it was during the period following this that Brian and I became close friends and spoke often together in person or on the telephone. Through days spent together I heard more and more of his and Stella's extraordinary life together.

Back in the mid-80s I read Norman Grubb's book "Rees Howells, Intercessor" and was gripped by the amazing testimony to the faithfulness of God which had led Rees Howells to become the totally devoted man of God he was. On a holiday when our children were young I recall visiting the College. I remember seeing a fleeting glimpse of Mr Samuel Howells, Rees's son and successor, but I have never forgotten meeting a quiet and unassuming man named David Davies who spent some time with us telling us about the College. David Davies had been a student at the college and then a missionary to the Congo where he had witnessed a powerful revival in 1954 and had miraculously escaped certain death during the Simba rebellion of 1964 when he and his wife were captives of the rebels. He had returned to lecture at the College and spent much of his time there and often spoke to visitors. He was a man who was steeped in prayer and made a deep impression on all who knew him.

I mention him because in many ways Brian Halliwell reminds me very much of him. The Bible College of Wales is in Brian's blood but not just in a reminiscent or romanticised way but because it was there that he and Stella wholly surrendered their lives to their Lord; where Stella was so gloriously baptised in the Holy Spirit and then supremely because of a day, documented in this book, when the glory of God came down on the College in the most remarkable way – an experience that has remained with Brian all his life and which continues to inspire him to prayer and intercession. His longing is not a self-interested thirst after experience but that the body of God's people might once again know the reality of God's presence among them when His glory is revealed.

I have much to thank God for because of Brian's faithfulness in prayer for me and my family and only eternity will reveal the effectiveness and consequences of this man's ongoing intercession - as is the case with so many other of God's precious people. Most of them are unknown and unsung heroes in this world but not in the courts of heaven, the only place that counts.

Many times and on many occasions you will read in this book that the Lord spoke to Brian and to Stella – sometimes individually, often together. To secular and even many Christian ears that claim will sound either strange or even unbelievable. Nevertheless it is true. Brian told me that one day driving Mr Samuel Howells on a trip to Brynaman and the Black Mountains Brian asked him, "How do you know for certain when it is God who is speaking to you?" Mr Samuel replied simply (using a Welsh term of endearment), "You'll know, bach." Brian and Stella proved that many times. After all, our Saviour tells us clearly in John 10:27, "My sheep hear My voice, and I know them, and they follow." I pray that you too will hear the voice of the Good Shepherd in the pages of this book as Brian recounts his testimony of not only hearing but also responding in obedience to His voice and His leading and guiding.

The great appeal of Rees Howells' testimony is the remarkable way that he was led to lead a life of faith completely dependent on God's provision from the smallest thing to the greatest. Most of the students and staff of the Bible College of Wales followed his example. Brian and Stella Halliwell's story is also of a testimony to a life of faith utterly dependent on God's provision. Nothing was ever asked for, but what was needed was prayed for and God never let them down. Having laid their all on the altar at the beginning of their journey of faith they were never salaried and yet never in want. They may not have been called to buy mansions and establish Bible colleges and schools, but they were called to establish Christian bookshops throughout Chile, in Peru and in the United Kingdom. Only eternity will reveal the extent of their service to the Kingdom of God in this world.

Finally, this book was a joy to write for many reasons but mainly for the blessing of the times that we sat down with a voice recorder and Brian shared with me his memories of Stella and their life and service together. I have tried where possible to remain faithful to his words.

I would also like to acknowledge the many people who read the draft of this book and who provided constructive criticism and comments. I would particularly thank Jane Gregor who kindly proof read the draft and apart from more technical amendments also gave me some helpful suggestions.

Finally I sing along with Brian and Stella's favourite hymn, "To God be the glory, great things He hath done."

David Jones. 2016

Preface

For some time I have wanted to write a book about my dear wife and partner Stella and our lives together. She was truly God's provision for me and who I am today is the result of how Father God used her to make me a stronger person and to have the confidence in myself to fulfil His work.

When Stella went to be with her Lord and Saviour in 2014 it was exactly 50 years since the time when we stepped out in faith and gave everything to the Lord by laying it on the altar. That happened in 1964 in the Bible College of Wales through the ministry of Duncan Campbell.

We stepped out in service for God, to work for his purposes and the extension of His Kingdom on earth. Over all these years we have experienced the guidance and provision of God for every situation, seeking to do His will for our lives, stepping out in faith in each different situation. We could never say that it has been dull or uninteresting through all the 50 years we had together in His service.

I will give you a brief summary, up to the time of Stella's death in 2014:

- We had both lived through the Second World War.
- We had both known Jesus as our Saviour for 55 years.
- We had been married for 53 years.
- We had moved 25 times during our married life.
- We had been 40 years together in CLC ministry.
- We had worked and lived in five different countries.
- We had worked and lived in fifteen different cities.
- We had set up nine new CLC bookstores.

- We had refitted six old CLC bookstores.
- We had managed five of those bookstores for CLC.

And to add to all of that, we also helped fit six other bookstores outside of our mission and we pastored a church for nearly two years in Andover.

As you will see, it is quite impossible to put all this down in writing. So I have chosen those parts that I feel could be a blessing and a help to you the reader. I trust it will lead you to knowing the Lord Jesus Christ as your Saviour and you too will know and fulfil His will in your life.

May Father God richly bless you as you read this book. To God be the glory, great things He hath done.

Brian A. Halliwell

1. Stella's Early Life.

Stella Marion Halliwell (nee Wilson) was born on the 29th of June 1938, in Upper Norwood, London. She was the second of two children born to William and Evelyn Wilson. Her brother Johnnie was 18 months older than her. Her father, who was known as Bill, was the only surviving child of twins born to an unmarried mother. Bill had fathered a child out of wedlock seven years before marrying Evelyn and because this was frowned upon in those days, Evelyn's mother found it difficult to accept Bill as her son-in-law. Not only did these circumstances mean that Bill and Evelyn had a difficult life at the beginning of their marriage, but also because the Second World War was looming this was not a happy time for the family. Bill was called up into the army and Evelyn was left at home alone to care for the children.

Figure 1 Evelyn Madge Wilson

Life was hard and dangerous in London during the Blitz and Stella later recalled the many times that she and Johnnie had to get under the kitchen table during bombing raids. Thankfully, the worst thing that happened was that on one occasion their front door was blown off.

Figure 2 Evelyn with Stella in her arms and Bill holding Johnnie

Evelyn's health deteriorated rapidly during the war years and sadly she developed tuberculosis and died in 1944. Johnnie and Stella were six and five respectively at the time. Stella's last memory of their mother was in the kitchen coughing up blood over the kitchen sink. Evelyn was rushed off to hospital where she died shortly after.

Bill was given compassionate leave to return home in order to be with Stella and Johnnie and to decide how they could best be cared for. In later life Bill told Stella that at that time, while he was on leave, he went to a gospel meeting taken by a well-known evangelist of that time called Gipsy Smith[1]. At the end of the meeting Bill responded to the appeal and accepted Jesus Christ as his Saviour.

Now Bill's immediate need was to know how to provide care for the children. He called at a local minister's house to ask for advice, but sad to say he was turned away by the minister. As he left disappointed, he decided that if the minister represented the church's attitude to those in need, then he would find his own way through life and turned his back on his new-found faith.

So Bill had to decide what was best for Johnnie and Stella. He was still in the army and the war was still on and he had to return to duty, so the only course of action open to him was to turn to relatives for help. Because of the rejection he had suffered from his in-laws in the past, he did not want to ask Evelyn's family to care for the children although they were willing and able to do so. Instead, he turned to his own relatives for help.

He took Johnnie and Stella up to Preston to stay with his mother. She lived in a "two up, two down" terraced house and was very poor. She was already caring for Bill's son who had been born out of wedlock before his marriage to Evelyn. He was ten years older than Stella and therefore about fifteen at the time. The two young children stayed there for a short time but Bill's mother struggled to cope with three children and it was suggested that Stella be sent to Blackburn to Bill's cousin Herbert and his wife Florrie. They had no children of their own and they were willing and wanted to adopt her.

With the war still going on, Bill, who by now was based back in London, realised that he had little choice and consented to Stella's adoption by Herbert and Florrie. Obviously this meant a big change for Stella who now had to be parted from her brother Johnnie. On 24th October, 1944,

Bill went up to Blackburn to sign adoption papers. Stella was six years old at that time, and it must have been a very disorientating and difficult time for her. It was also a difficult time for Bill – but he really had little alternative.

Figure 3 Herbert and Florrie's Home, Blackburn (more recent photo)

When the war came to an end and Bill came out of the army, he married again and settled down to live in Croydon. At that time Johnnie left his grandmother's home in Preston and went to live with his dad and his new wife, Nellie.

Figure 4 Stella

Stella remained in Blackburn with her stepfather and stepmother, Herbert and Florrie Shorrock. Also living with them was Herbert's mother Annie, who actually was Bill's aunt (his mother's sister) and thus Stella's great aunt. Now Annie became known to Stella as Grandma Annie by adoption. Herbert and Florrie both had full-time jobs in the cotton mill, so it fell to Annie to look after Stella. They became very close and Stella grew to love her adoptive grandmother very much.

She also grew to love her adoptive parents, Herbert and Florrie, who cared and looked after her very well. They all lived in a lovely terraced house in Blackburn and Herbert also owned the house next door. On a few occasions Annie would go to Preston to visit her sister, Bill's mother and of course Stella's actual grandmother, and would take Stella with her. That meant that before Johnnie moved to London, Stella was able to spend a little time with her brother. At first Herbert was not too happy about these visits, being concerned that Stella might become unsettled. However, knowing that Johnnie would soon be returning to his father in Croydon, he allowed the visits to go on.

Figure 5 Florrie and Herbert Shorrock, Stella and Annie

And so Stella grew up in Blackburn attending the local schools. Her ambition was to become a nurse when she finished her education at fifteen, but was told she was too young and she was asked to apply again when she was eighteen. She then started work in a baker's shop and continued her education by attending night school. But after a year or so, not being happy at the bakery, she went to work in a slipper factory where she found that she could earn more money.

Figure 6 Florrie, Stella, Annie and Herbert on a day out.

Herbert and Florrie were not regular churchgoers but allowed Stella to attend St Andrews Anglican Church which was only five minutes from their home. Stella became very much involved in the church, working with the Sunday School and Girl Guides. She also had a close friend called Betty Holt whose mother was a born-again Christian and longed and prayed to see God move among the young people of St Andrews Church. Then at the age of eighteen, Stella made a commitment which would change her life. Here is Stella's testimony taken from her note book.

"When I was at the age of eighteen, the church held a Church Army campaign led by a group that came up from London. During that time I went to a house group meeting at Mrs Holt's home. It was taken by a Church Army officer. At the end of the meeting when I was leaving, the officer asked me, 'Are you a Christian?' Taken by surprise, I answered, 'Well, I attend the church each week, teach in the Sunday School, and work with the Girl Guides and help where I can in the church. I would say yes.' The officer gently replied, 'That does not make you a Christian.' I then went straight out of the door. What the officer had said really upset me and made me unsettled and angry but I decided to go and hear the team again at the church that weekend.

"I went along that Sunday evening with a friend. When the time came to hear the message, I found the theme was the cross. It was then my spiritual eyes were opened and I understood what it was all about. It was not because of anything I had done that made me a child of God, but it was about what Jesus had done at Calvary for me. It was then that I saw that He took all my sin, guilt and shame upon Himself and dealt with it once and for all on that cross. He took on Himself the wrath of God which I deserved. Yes, He took my place upon that cross.

"I just felt then that I had to get out of my seat and go forward when the appeal was made. But then I began to wonder what my friend would think of me. I just had to get past her. I then went out to the front in repentance and coming before the Throne of Grace and I said, 'Lord, please forgive me for what I am. I accept that you offered yourself for me and that you are my Lord and Saviour.' I felt such a cleansing. I knew that I was born again of the Holy Spirit and was now a child of God.

"A few weeks later I went down with a number of other Christians to the Church Army H.Q. in London for a long weekend. It was a great time of fellowship and sharing. It was wonderful to be able to give my testimony on Speakers' Corner in Hyde Park. That was a great experience. I just did not want the fellowship we had to end. It was such a wonderful time. When I went back to the church of St Andrews my life took on a new purpose in serving my Lord and Saviour Jesus Christ."

It is worth noting at this point that the notebook in which Stella wrote this testimony was later used by the Lord to bring Stella and Brian together.

Figure 7 Stella in her teens

Stella was confirmed in St Andrews Anglican Church in Blackburn and continued to worship there.

Figure 8 Stella at her confirmation

2. Brian's Early Life

Brian Halliwell was born on 1st June, 1939, just months before the start of World War II in a town called Darwen, Lancashire, four miles away from Blackburn, where Stella lived with her adoptive parents. Like Stella, he too was the younger of two children. His father Albert ran a plumbing and maintenance business which he had inherited from his father. He had a number of men working for him and a great deal of his work was for local mills in that part of Lancashire.

Figure 9 Albert Halliwell (right) with his team of plumbers on a day out

Brian was a sickly child. During his early years he contracted double pneumonia and almost died. His father later told him that it was through people's prayers for him that he pulled through. Brian's family were not religious, but God-fearing. His dad often knelt at the side of the bed with him and taught him how to pray.

When he was about four years old it was found that he had a problem with his hearing. He also developed festering sores and scabs on the palm of his right hand which would not heal. Self-conscious of this and not wanting people to see his hand, he often wore a glove on it. His parents took him to see a number of doctors but they could not determine what the cause of the problem was.

In junior school around the age of five, he was dared by a fellow scholar to make a small tear in a table cloth. He made the small tear but then was promptly reported by the same boy. As a result he was caned in spite of the obvious scarring on his hand. This incident prompted Brian's dad to take him out of school and arrange private education with an Irish lady called Miss Regan. With just eighteen pupils in his class, Brian flourished.

Figure 10 Young Brian

But then Brian had to go into hospital to have a lump removed from his shoulder. While he was in hospital the sores on his hand were noticed and arrangements were made for him to see a doctor. However, in the meantime a church visitor came to the ward and spoke to Brian and asked him if he would mind if he prayed for him. Brian agreed and, as the visitor was leaving, he gave Brian a New Testament. Brian put it under his pillow and went to sleep.

When he woke up he found to his amazement that the sores on his hand had dried up and soon the scabs began to drop off and within a day or so they had all gone leaving only scars. Brian knew the Lord had healed him from a condition he'd suffered with for a number of years. From that time onwards Brian always carried a small New Testament or Bible in his pocket wherever he went

Figure 11 The house where Brian grew up in Darwen

When he was about seven or eight another incident had a lasting impact on Brian's life. He and his brother Roy, who was four years older, were out walking on the moors near Darwen with their dog. They were above an old quarry known as Blue Delve. The dog went near the edge of the quarry and when Roy moved to get him, he slipped and fell some 60 feet, just missing a big boulder at the edge of the water below. Young Brian didn't know what to do and couldn't get down to his brother, but he went to the edge and knelt down and prayed and asked God for His help. He remembers saying that if God did this for him he would commit himself to God.

He ran home to tell his mother what had happened. He learned afterwards that a couple had been having a picnic on the opposite side of the quarry, had seen what had happened and had run to a nearby farmhouse to call an ambulance. Roy sustained head injuries and was taken to Blackburn Royal Infirmary unconscious. He made a good recovery but the injuries were serious enough to prevent him from being conscripted into the army for National Service when he became old enough. The quarry was later fenced off.

When Brian was ten his father arranged for him to attend the junior section of Blackburn Grammar School to be prepared for the 11-plus examination. He subsequently passed the examination and attended the Grammar School. But at the age of twelve more ill health intervened and Brian developed tuberculosis of the kidney. The GP wanted his father to admit him to hospital to have the infected kidney removed, but it so happened that at that time streptomycin was becoming available. Brian was put on a six-month course of the new antibiotic – one of the first persons to be treated with it. He recovered but was out of school for over two years and eventually went back for just the last six months of his schooling.

During this period out of school Brian learned practical skills from his father when he could. He melted old solder, skimmed it and poured it into moulds to make solder sticks for re-use. He learned how to make and plumb solder joints. As a result of the bombing of the area around Darwen during the war, there was a demand for replacement glass in factories and homes. So his father had branched out into the re-glazing business and Brian recalls seeing glass being delivered by train from Pilkington, the glass manufacturer, and learning how to cut glass. He even taught himself how to make glass art. His dad also did electrical work which Brian attempted to learn but found more difficult because, in addition to his other problems, he was colour-blind and could not distinguish between red and green, which of course meant that electrical work was not for him.

Brian always spoke very fondly of his dad who spent a great deal of time with him, helping him to learn all manner of practical skills which became invaluable later in his life. Brian also helped his father to keep the accounts, prepare invoices and also helped to do the payroll, assisting another family member who did the job full-time.

Figure 12 Brian and Roy with their parents, Albert and Dorothy Halliwell

As a result of his work as a plumber, Brian's father Albert developed lead poisoning and was admitted to Buxton Hospital for some six months. While he was away the business lost customers and money. Some of his employees took advantage of his absence to do jobs on the side, using materials belonging to the business. When Albert was discharged he was able to continue with the business for a short time but then Roy, Brian's older brother, took charge of it and began to rebuild it.

In 1954 at the age of fifteen, Brian left school and wanted to go into his father's business with his brother, but because of his past illnesses doctors advised his father against it. So Albert asked a friend, who was a master butcher, to take Brian on and teach him the trade. Brian started work in the Darwen Co-operative butchery department. He grew to enjoy the work but because of his poor hearing he struggled when it came to dealing with customers.

Brian decided he would like to find a job doing the back-room work of the butchery trade, preparing different kinds of cooked meat and making different types of sausages. This would mean he could avoid having to deal with customers. As he was going to work early one morning, carrying his New Testament in his pocket, he was thinking about Jesus and wondering whether He was really alive and whether the New Testament accounts were really true. So there and then he decided to ask Him and simply prayed, "Lord, if you're real, please reveal Yourself in some way to me." That evening he was looking through the local newspaper at job vacancies and found that a firm of German pork butchers, who had their own abattoir and shop in Blackburn, were advertising for a butcher. The firm specialised in various kinds of cooked meats and sausages and the work was just what Brian wanted. He applied for the job and was successful.

He worked with a Christian man called Frank Ainsworth, who was an elder in the local Brethren Church. Frank used to witness to Brian about what Jesus had done for him and urged Brian to commit his life to the Lord. This went on for a number of weeks until finally one day he told Brian that he wouldn't keep on trying to persuade him but would leave him to think about one final simple question, "What will you do with Jesus? Will you accept Him or reject Him?" Brian remembers clearly that this happened while they were working in the back room of the shop as he was cutting up a side of beef! He shouted, "I'll accept Him."

What he had said didn't really have an impact on him until he got home that night, got out his Bible and read through Matthew's Gospel. It was then that the Word of God began to come alive to him and it was at that point he saw and understood what Jesus had done for Him on the cross. Right there and then he prayed and repented of his sin and was born again of the Holy Spirit.

The next day he told Frank Ainsworth what he had done and the two of them rejoiced and shared often with one another. Within two weeks Brian was baptised in water following a campaign at the Elim Hall Brethren assembly in Blackburn and came into fellowship in the Church. He attended the Church for six months. So Brian, like Stella, had come to know the Lord as his Saviour at around the same time. They were both eighteen when they became Christians.

Figure 13 Elim Hall Brethren Church in Blackburn where Brian was baptised. Stella was also baptised there later.

As well as Elim Hall, Blackburn, Brian also attended the Brethren church in Darwen occasionally, where he got to know one of the elders, Mr Grundy, who tried to persuade him to go to Bible College. Although Brian did not respond at the time, he remembered Mr Grundy's words and ultimately they proved to be prophetic.

Brian's father had lost much of his savings during his illness but he still owned his own house, so he sold up and bought a butcher's shop with living accommodation. At the age of nineteen Brian left his job in Blackburn with the German pork butchers and ran his own shop in Darwen. He bought an old Jowett Javelin van which had a horizontal air-cooled engine, and in addition to the shop he branched into selling pre-packed meat, which was quite a pioneering move at the time. He took the meats around various shops where it would be kept at the top of their ice-cream fridges until sold.

Figure 14 Brian's Jowett Javelin van

This move and other distractions resulted in him backsliding and not attending church for some two years. Looking back, he admits that he had not only neglected church, but he also began to neglect his business. As far as church was concerned, his poor hearing hadn't helped. The church had a hearing-aid system and while it was available for the morning communion services, Brian struggled to hear clearly and felt that he couldn't participate in the meetings.

He also started going to dances and, being naturally shy, he started taking a drink or two before going - for Dutch courage. However, the drinking increased. He started dating a Catholic girl and his neglect of his butchery business eventually led to him having to close the shop. The family moved into a flat and rented out the shop. The girl that he had fallen for eventually broke off the relationship.

Brian then got a job working as a butcher for a big local bakery in Blackburn, buying beef and pork and preparing cooked meats for them to sell in the shop. It was during this period that he met Stella. This meeting was to change both their lives and lead to a future that neither of them could have imagined at the time.

3. Brian and Stella

In September 1960 Brian had become increasingly unhappy and aware that he was missing the fellowship of Church. He was very conscious of what the Lord had done for him and wanted to go back, but was afraid to do so. He prayed and asked the Lord to find him a Christian girl to help him.

One Saturday night he went to the dance hall with his friends. He had the last dance of the night with one of the girls and then went to the exit to wait for his friends. The girl who he had just danced with walked by and as she passed him he seemed to hear the Lord say to him, "That's the girl I have for you."

On the following weekend he met her once again and this time he was determined to walk her home. He asked her for the last dance and at the end of it he offered to see her home and she accepted. When they got to her home she asked Brian if he would like to come in and have a coffee. Brian accepted without hesitation. They got into conversation and he began to ask her about herself. He then asked her whether she knew Jesus as her Saviour. Stella didn't say anything immediately but went to a drawer, pulled out a notebook and said to him, "Read that while I make the coffee."

Brian could hardly believe what he was reading (this was the notebook in which Stella had written down her testimony after committing her life to Jesus). The Lord said to him, "Didn't I tell you that she was the one." Stella came in with the coffees with a smile on her face. They both sensed very early on that they were meant for each other and that was the beginning of their courtship.

3. Brian and Stella

Ten days later, Brian took Stella to see the film *The Ten Commandments*. They went back to her home that evening. He told her quite honestly and openly, "You are the sort of girl I would like to marry." With that she started to cry. He asked her what was wrong and she replied, "It's not every day that someone proposes to me." Brian then realised that although he hadn't intended it she had taken his words as a proposal and he was thrilled that she had accepted it as such. He had no doubts that this was meant to be.

Stella carried on attending the Anglican Church, but they also began worshipping together. They attended Youth for Christ meetings on Saturday nights and got involved in nights of prayer. Brian sold his van and worked hard to clear the debt that he had got himself into. Stella had a good job which paid well in a local slipper factory.

And then something happened, which was to leave a lasting impression on Brian. He left Stella's house late one evening and set out to walk the four miles home to Darwen. As he arrived there around midnight, the Lord spoke to him and told him to go to the home of the elderly Mr Grundy, the elder in the Darwen Brethren Church, who had earlier tried to persuade Brian to consider going to Bible College. He lived about thirty minutes away at the other end of the town. Brian had not seen Mr Grundy for almost two years – since he had stopped attending church.

Brian started out without question and about halfway there, the Lord spoke again to him saying, "He wants to see you because he is dying." Arriving at the end of the street at one o'clock in the morning, Brian began to have doubts and remembers thinking, "Surely this can't be right – perhaps I'm just imagining this." He saw a car outside Mr Grundy's house, and it occurred to him that it might be the doctor. He waited until the car left and then got up courage to knock at the door. A lady opened the door. He asked if it was possible to see Mr

Grundy. She replied, "I'm sorry it's not possible, he is very ill." Brian began to cry and the lady, feeling sorry for him, asked him into the house and took him into the front room where Mr Grundy lay in bed.

When he saw Brian for the first time for over two years, he sat up in bed with a smile on his face. He was full of joy to see him because he had continued to pray for him. Brian told him about Stella and his renewed commitment to faith. Mr Grundy was delighted and after spending some precious time together, Brian left the house early in the morning. The following Tuesday Mr Grundy died and went to be with his Lord.

Six months after their first meeting, Brian and Stella were married on 25th March, 1961, at the church that Stella had grown up in, St Andrews in Blackburn.

Figure 15 Stella on her wedding day

It was a lovely and precious time for Stella, because her adoptive mother Florrie allowed her birth father to give her away at the wedding (her adoptive father Herbert Shorrock had died at the comparatively young age of 54 in 1956). Bill travelled up from London and walked her down the aisle. The couple were able to buy a three-bedroomed gabled house in Blackburn with the help of Brian's father who arranged for them to obtain a full mortgage on the property. They started attending the Elim Hall Brethren assembly in Blackburn together where Stella was baptised in water and where they both grew in their Christian faith and commitment.

They also began helping with a Christian work started by a lady called Mrs Lamont. She and her husband had opened their home to girls who had ended up in prostitution in Blackburn and had no home to go to. Realising the value of this work, the local council had offered to buy the house next door so that the two houses could be converted into one in order to create further accommodation for girls. The local police started bringing destitute young girls to Mrs Lamont for help and this prompted the council to go further and offer her the use of a former nurses' accommodation block. Brian and Stella's involvement in this work was to go on for many years. Brian, who had learned so many skills with his father, did a lot of the conversion work on the buildings and they both worked alongside Mrs Lamont.

Figure 16 Brian and Stella's home in Blackburn

They also became involved with an interdenominational mission called Message of Victory Evangelism (M.O.V.E.) led by a Mr and Mrs Harvey.[2] The work and organisation was similar in many respects to the Salvation Army. The workers wore a brown uniform and visited local pubs and clubs, selling a Christian magazine and inviting anyone who would come to a late-night meeting in the centre of Blackburn where testimonies and a simple gospel message were shared.

Stella loved hairdressing and was persuaded by a relative that she should take it up professionally. She applied to the Kendal Miller School of Hairdressing in Preston and was accepted on a six-month course. This was a prestigious hairdressing school at the time and well-known for bringing young hairdressers up to competition standard. Stella was quick to learn and Brian recalls that at an awards ceremony at the end of the course the popular singer Engelbert Humperdinck came along to sing and to present the awards.

Brian converted the large front room at their home into a salon for Stella. When they had married, Stella's stepmother Florrie had hoped that the couple would go to live with her, but when they didn't she asked Stella if she would care for her adoptive grandmother Annie. Brian agreed and so Annie went to live with them. Annie kindly loaned the couple some money to help them to set up the salon. They bought three hairdryers and some seating, and Stella began her new career. She and Brian hand-delivered some fliers round the area and the salon was opened on the 5th April, 1962. Stella was a talented hairdresser and it didn't take long for her to gain a great reputation. Soon the salon was doing really well – so well that Stella ended up working long hours.

Figure 17 Stella with her aunt in front of the hairdressing salon

4. The Challenge

Figure 18 Annie, Stella's adoptive grandmother

Stella's grandmother Annie died in December 1963. Brian and Stella had continued to worship at the local Brethren Church where Stella became involved with the children's work. Now as they prayed together and individually they felt that God was calling them to full-time ministry either with M.O.V.E or alongside Mrs Lamont. Either way, they both felt that God was challenging them to sell up and go into full-time service for Him.

They went up to the Lake District to a M.O.V.E. convention where they shared their heart with Mr and Mrs Harvey, the founders of M.O.V.E. in Britain. They met before the meeting and Mr Harvey suggested that they go into the meeting, which by now had started, and he prayed that God would speak to them through the meeting and the message. The Bible reading was the gospel story of the rich young ruler to whom Jesus said, "Go your way, sell whatever you have and give to the poor, and you will have treasure in heaven; and come, take up the cross, and follow Me" (Mark 10:21). This message had a powerful impact on both Brian and Stella. It not only challenged them, but also confirmed what God had been speaking to them about individually and together.

Around this time Brian took a friend, who was thinking of applying to go to Bible College, on a visit to the Birmingham Bible Institute. But things didn't work out for his friend who eventually decided not to go. But the Lord used this visit to speak into Brian's heart saying, "I want you to go to Bible college". Remembering Mr Grundy's words and having prayed about this, Brian and Stella wrote to the Glasgow Bible Training Institute which had an excellent reputation at that time. In a letter to the principal, they explained the Lord's call upon their lives, how He had prospered them and how they were prepared to be obedient to His call to sell up and follow Him into Christian service. Disappointingly for them, the principal wrote back to say that he didn't feel that they were doing the right thing and that they should use their prosperity to support others already in full-time ministry.

So in July 1964 Brian and Stella decided to take a holiday while they thought and prayed about the way forward. They hired a Bedford Dormobile campervan and planned to visit the west coast of Scotland, travelling up to Fort William. However, the Lord had different plans for them and the week before the holiday, a typhoid epidemic was reported in Scotland and people were advised to avoid holidays there. So they changed their plans and decided to tour Wales instead.

While they were part of the M.O.V.E. mission in Blackburn, they had met and spent time with Rowland[3] and Ann Evans who were the leaders in the Welsh branch of the mission. They lived at Llanelli in West Wales and so they decided to visit them and then have a holiday touring Wales. Brian had also heard about the Bible College of Wales in Swansea and, being curious, thought it worthwhile to visit it. They spent a day in Llanelli and having obtained directions from Rowland, they travelled on to Swansea.

Figure 19 Brian kept this original brochure for the Dormobile they hired.

They followed the directions, but when they arrived in the vicinity of Derwen Fawr[4], the house and estate that was the main hub of the College, Brian couldn't see any sign of it. Then he saw an elderly lady coming through a gate and winding down the campervan window, he enquired whether she knew where the Bible College of Wales was. "You're here," she replied. She turned out to be Miss Williams, one of the staff at the College. She asked why they wanted to know and Brian explained that they'd heard about the College and they were curious to see it and find out more about it. It was around lunchtime and Miss Williams invited them to join the staff and students for lunch.

They parked their campervan in Sketty Isaf, one of the other College properties nearby, were shown into the dining room in Derwen Fawr House and sat down to lunch opposite Mr Samuel Howells, the Director of the College. Mr Samuel, as he was known to all at the College, was the son of Mr and Mrs Rees Howells. Rees Howells had been the founder and first director of the College.

After lunch they were shown around the house and then taken down to Glynderwen, just down the road towards the sea, the first estate which Rees Howells had been led to buy and where the College had been first established. Glynderwen was then the home of Emmanuel Grammar and Preparatory School. There they met "Uncle Tommy" - Tommy Howells, who had been a close friend and prayer partner of Rees Howells (not a relative). Uncle Tommy took them around Glynderwen and gave them a copy of Norman Grubb's book entitled *Rees Howells, Intercessor*, which tells the story of the life and ministry of the College founder. During their conversation Uncle Tommy also mentioned that a Christian conference was beginning at the College on the following Saturday.

From Swansea Brian and Stella travelled up to North Wales, reading the book to each other wherever they stayed each night. The book made a huge impression on them and as they read it together the Lord began speaking to them about the work of the Holy Spirit and His ministry in the life of Rees Howells.

On the Sunday they were in Caernarvon and decided that they'd like to attend church. They had some difficulty finding an English church, the area being predominantly Welsh speaking. But then they spotted a notice outside a building advertising an English service to be held on the first floor of the building that evening. They decided they would go and returned in time to attend the service. In the event, they were the only people there apart from the pastor and his wife. They introduced themselves and it turned out that the pastor had a connection to M.O.V.E. which made them feel at home.

4. The Challenge

They learned that the pastor was used to a small congregation but however many turned up he would preach anyway with the windows wide open so that passers-by could overhear. He had no idea that Brian and Stella had been praying about the ministry and Baptism of the Holy Spirit but that evening he spoke on Acts chapter 2 and at the end of the service offered to pray with them that they might receive the Baptism of the Holy Spirit. Brian recalls that as he was prayed for he felt a remarkable impartation of faith and knew in his spirit that his prayer had been heard and answered.

They decided to travel back down south so that they could get to the Bible College by the following Sunday for the first day of the "Every Creature" conference. This was an annual interdenominational conference begun by Rees Howells in 1947 after the Second World War when national and international speakers would be invited to come to the College to speak. It took its name from the Lord's commission to His disciples that they should "Go into all the world and preach the gospel to every creature" (Mark 16:15), and from the vision for world evangelism that the Lord had given to Rees Howells on Boxing Day morning in 1934.[5]

Brian and Stella spent the week travelling down the west coast of Wales and arrived in Swansea on the Saturday. Having found a place to stay, they made their way to the Bible College on the Sunday morning for the opening session. On that morning they heard three of the guest speakers and after an afternoon break they attended the evening service when Duncan Campbell[6] was the speaker. He was a man whom God had used mightily in the Hebrides Revival, which flourished between 1949 and 1952, and was a regular visitor to the College. His theme that evening was God's call to lay everything on the altar and serve Him - total surrender. This was a significant and powerful message, particularly for Stella who responded immediately at the end of the service together with Brian. This was a further confirmation that the Lord was calling them both to sell up all that they had and follow Him full-time.

Figure 20 Duncan Campbell at the Bible College of Wales.

The couple travelled back to Blackburn on that Sunday night so that Stella could open the hairdressing salon on the Monday because she had to fulfil previously-arranged appointments. Brian didn't have a regular job to go to (he was helping in the hairdresser's at that time), but as he spent time in prayer that day he felt that the Lord wanted him to return to Swansea for the remainder of the conference. He shared this with Stella who selflessly encouraged him to go even though she couldn't go herself. So he went back to Swansea by train on the Tuesday to attend the conference for the rest of the week.

At the College he saw Mr Samuel Howells who said that one of the speakers, the international evangelist Leonard

Ravenhill, was leaving and that Brian could make use of the room in the men's hostel for the conference duration. Although Brian had no idea who Leonard Ravenhill was at the time, he remembers that he did spend some time with him.

It was during this conference week that God confirmed that He wanted Brian to enrol at the Bible College of Wales. He was reminded of his experience some years before when Mr Grundy, the Brethren elder, had so encouraged him to think about attending Bible College. The disappointment of being turned down for the Glasgow Bible Training Institute turned to joy and peace as Brian realised the direction his life was taking. Excited and full of all that God had done and spoken during the conference meetings, Brian returned to Blackburn anxious to share his heart with Stella.

However, after spending time in prayer together, Stella felt that she didn't have the witness that this was something that God wanted her to do at that time. But she saw and understood how sure Brian was about his call and she gladly encouraged and released Brian to be obedient to it. Brian naturally felt disappointed - he had hoped that they would go to college together - but also he was confident that this was definitely what the Lord wanted for him. Brian immediately sent off an application to the College.

During this time back in Blackburn Brian recalls sharing a little of his experience at Caernarvon with another Brethren couple who were of a similar age to him and Stella. The couple asked if they could share a time of prayer together and Brian and Stella willingly agreed. The wife suffered with a very bad back and during the prayer time Brian suddenly had a vision of the cross and it seemed as though fire was burning into him and the Lord was telling him to speak into her life and to pray for her healing. He'd never done anything like that before and resisted. He was conscious that she had been to Bible college and he saw her as far more experienced than he was. However, the more he resisted, the more the flames persisted until he could contain himself no longer but burst out that he had to pray for her. He did so and she was healed. This was Brian's first experience of ministering to someone in the power of the Holy Spirit.

When they returned home that evening, Brian and Stella went to their bedroom to thank the Lord for His goodness to them. While Brian was at the side of the bed praying, he suddenly began to worship the Lord in tongues for the first time. Although Stella had not experienced that personal baptism in her own life, she continued to long for it, confident that in God's perfect time she too would be filled.

During the period between their return from holiday and Brian leaving for college, the couple continued to attend the Brethren church in Blackburn. Brian shared his experience of the Baptism in the Holy Spirit with some of the members, but although they did not ask them to leave the church they also made it clear that this wasn't something of which they approved. In general the Brethren churches along with others do not recognise that Baptism in the Spirit is a separate experience from conversion.

Brian and Stella prepared to sell the house and the business. They had comparatively little time to get things settled before the start of the College term and in fact Brian recalls that the whole enterprise seemed almost impossible at the time. They had cleared their mortgage but realised that because of the change of use of the building, whoever wanted to buy the business would not be able to obtain a mortgage but would have to get a bank loan which might make selling the business difficult. They prayed about it and advertised the business for two nights in the local press.

They had two responses. The first couple who came looked at the property but ultimately weren't interested. The second couple that came along loved the house and the business and when advised that they might have to get a bank loan in order to buy it said that this was no problem and that the whole amount required was already arranged and would be provided by the lady's aunt. So in God's providence the house sale went through quickly. Stella and Brian were amazed and praised God for His providence.

Now the couple had to find a home for Stella for the time that Brian was away at college. This wasn't so easy because at the time rented properties were very difficult to come by in Blackburn, and time was short as Brian had only weeks to go before he started college. But again, the Lord provided. Mr Harvey, the M.O.V.E. leader, contacted them to let them know that some M.O.V.E. workers, who were living in a rented house in Blackburn, were moving on to a different town and Brian and Stella should be able to rent the place that they were vacating. The property was a little two up, two down terraced house in Addison Street, Blackburn with no hot water, an outside toilet and flagstone floors. Although Brian didn't realise it at the time it was also in an area of Blackburn which was known as a red-light district. In spite of Brian's concerns, Stella insisted that the house would be fine and so they rented it.

All in all, what had seemed impossible had happened. The house and business were sold and in the week before Brian was due to leave for college, the couple had moved what furniture Stella needed to the house in Addison Street and the new owners had moved into the their old home. Brian had also sold their car. Stella needed a job and the rented house was near to a bakery and confectioners where Stella had worked previously. Her old boss offered her a job in the shop. Everything just fell into place under the providence of the Lord.

Figure 21 The rented house in Addison Street taken years later.

When they had moved into the house in Addison Street, they found that there was an Assemblies of God church nearby and they started going there. The pastor was very kind to Stella and after Brian left for BCW she began a children's group meeting in her home and it really took off. Brian recalls many wonderful things happening through this group, including children coming along whose parents were parting from each other and through prayer with the children the parents were reconciled.

Before Brian left for college, he and Stella asked the Lord what they should do with all the money from the sale of the house and the Lord showed them individually that when all was settled they should hand it to Mr Samuel Howells at the Bible College to do with whatever the Lord directed him to do. In obedience to Rees Howells' "Every Creature" vision, Samuel Howells, like his father before him, distributed funds regularly to numerous missions all over the world as the Lord directed him. The College ran entirely on the lines of faith which Rees Howells had established from the beginning. When there was a need identified, Samuel and the College staff and students would pray that the need be met and the Lord provided through others who were open to His prompting. No money was ever asked for from anyone, but whatever was needed was always provided in answer to the prayer of faith.

For the coming year Stella had only the money that she earned at the shop. Brian, in line with the other students at the College would learn to live entirely in dependence on the Lord. And so began the first year of them living apart. In September 1964 Brian went off to Swansea to BCW on the train - very tearfully he remembers - and Stella remained in Blackburn.

5. Brian's First Year in College 1964/65

And so, in the autumn of 1964 Brian commenced his studies at the Bible College of Wales. On his arrival he was allocated a room in the men's hostel which he shared with a third-year student. The College course was basically two years' study with an optional third year for men or women who had a call into full-time ministry or missionary service.

Figure 22 Brian (back row, 3rd from right) with first-year students.

At the end of the first term, just before Christmas, Brian travelled back to Blackburn to spend Christmas with Stella at Addison Street. By this time the sale of their house had been finalised and the couple agreed that Brian should take a cheque for the proceeds back with him to College.

On his return to College he asked to see Mr Samuel Howells who at this time had his desk in the Blue Room[7] at Derwen Fawr - a room that during the Second World War had been the centre for prayer and intercession for Rees Howells and the staff who had remained at the College. Brian recalls that this was the only visit to the Blue Room that he experienced during his student days. He was invited in and handed the cheque to Mr Samuel Howells who was already aware of Brian's testimony and calling.

Figure 23 Students and staff of BCW 1964/5. Dr Symonds (centre front) flanked by Arthur Lewis and Ieuan Jones. Brian is standing in the centre in front row of male students.

During his second term at College Brian had an experience which has lived vividly in his memory all his life. Duncan Campbell had again visited the College and ministered over the weekend. He spoke on the Friday evening and the Saturday morning on how God had brought about the Hebridean revival of 1949. He continued to minister at two Sunday services.

His final message was given in the last meeting on the Monday morning in the chapel room at Derwen Fawr house where students and those members of staff who could be there were gathered. Suddenly at the end of his message, the glory of God came down and filled that room. Brian recalls that everyone was face down on the floor and such a sense of God's holiness and glory filled the room that all those present were conscious of their own sinfulness and began to weep in repentance as God's presence became overpowering in that place. Then just as suddenly Brian recalls what he could only describe as waves of cleansing coming over the room which turned their weeping into overwhelming joy and thankfulness. He testifies that he has never experienced anything like that since that day, but the recollection of that intense experience has remained with him and it still drives him to pray and intercede and long for the presence and the glory of God to come down in such power again upon His people.

For days afterwards the College seemed filled with joy and peace. It was as if something of what had happened in the Hebrides in 1949 had happened again at Derwen Fawr. It made a huge and lasting impression on Brian and all who were present.

Later in that first year Duncan Campbell visited the College once again and for some reason (Brian has no idea why) he asked Mr Samuel if he could meet with Brian. Mr Samuel approached Brian and told him that Duncan Campbell would like to see him in the Green Room at Derwen Fawr. Duncan Campbell asked Brian to share his testimony with him and then he prayed with him there. Brian treasures that memory although he can't remember to this day what Duncan Campbell prayed. But he does feel that the incident had great significance for him and for his future ministry first in prayer and then later into intercession.

God also spoke to Brian through Mr Black who was a South American Gospel missionary who visited the College and showed slides and spoke about Chile. It was during one of his talks that the Lord spoke to Brian and told him that Chile was where He wanted him to go. But Brian resisted this because he had in his mind a plan to return to Blackburn after college to work with Stella alongside Mrs Lamont whose work among the unfortunate girls forced into prostitution was continuing. But this call to Chile wouldn't go away and so he

5. Brian's First Year in College 1964/65

wrote to the South American Gospel Mission and asked them to send him their magazine. He decided that when he received the magazine he would search through it and if it contained anything about a couple being needed for Chile, he would take that as a confirmation of his calling.

The magazine came and Brian read through it, but there was nothing about a couple being wanted for Chile. He admits being relieved. However, that evening he went up to his room but then realised that he'd left his Bible in the library and so he went down to get it. On the table in the College library were many of the prayer letters that had been sent to the College from all over the world and as Brian was leaving, the Lord prompted him to read a letter that was lying on the top of the pile. He picked it up and took it back to his room. It was a personal, hand-written letter from Mr Black to the College asking for prayer specifically for a couple for the mission in Chile. Brian was stunned but admits he was still resisting. A week or so later he prayed and asked that if this was really the Lord's will, would He confirm it by providing someone who would help him learn Spanish.

There were also other lessons to learn apart from classes. Brian had kept sufficient money out of the proceeds from the sale of the house to see him through his first year in college, but during the second term the Lord challenged him about this.

The College still has a large plinth (recently restored) in the grounds on one side of which is inscribed "Jehovah Jireh"- "the Lord will provide" and on the other "Faith is Substance" - referring to Hebrews 11:1, which states, "Now faith is the substance of things hoped for, the evidence of things not seen." Faith in God's provision was the basis on which the Holy Spirit taught Rees Howells to live and on which the College was founded. Learning to live by prayer and faith was the essential principle which was encouraged in every student.

As part of their training, the students would be sent out on Sunday appointments to speak at churches far and near. The College had a minibus to take the students locally and it was the students' challenge to pray that sufficient funds would be provided to pay for tax and insurance and the running costs of the minibus.

At this time the minibus fund was in trouble and a certain sum was required in order to insure it. Dr Symonds was an ENT specialist who had devoted his life to the Lord and to the welfare of the male students at the College. He met with the students regularly for prayer. On this occasion he pointed out to them that the sum that was required was exactly the same amount as the number of great fish that were caught when the risen Jesus told His disciples to cast their net on the right side of the boat - one hundred and fifty three (John 21:1-11).

As they prayed, Brian suddenly realised that the sum of money required for the insurance was exactly what was left of the sum that he had kept back in order to provide for his first year. The Lord spoke clearly to Brian and simply said, "Don't ask Me for that which you can provide yourself." That night he learned a very important lesson. He gave the £153 that he had in order to pay for the minibus insurance and began to wholly depend on God for all his needs.

A further challenge came in his second term when, at their regular daily early morning devotions together, his room-mate prayed for a new pair of shoes. Brian had just one tidy pair but his room-mate's shoes were really in a bad state so they prayed that the Lord would provide for them both. Within a few days a parcel arrived at the College for Brian. Completely unsolicited, his brother Roy had sent him a brand new pair of shoes. He was overjoyed at this answer to prayer and thanked God for the provision. It occurred to him that since his room-mate took the same size shoes, he could now give him his old shoes which although worn were still in much better shape than the ones his room-mate had.

That night he went to bed and again the Lord spoke to him and asked him, "If I needed a pair of shoes which ones would you give to me?" Brian replied, "I'd give you the brand new pair, Lord." And the words of Jesus came to him, "Inasmuch as you did it to one of the least of these My brethren, you did it to Me" (Matthew 25:40). Brian got the message immediately and quietly left the brand-new pair on his room-mate's bed the following day and continued to wear his older pair.

But that was not the end of the matter for now there followed a further and unexpected lesson. That very weekend Brian was sent to Treorchy in the Rhondda Valley to speak on the Sunday. He travelled up on the Saturday and went to the house of the couple who were hosting him for the weekend.

After dinner that evening the husband proposed a walk through the town and as they walked he stopped at a shop, unlocked the door and invited Brian to come in. "This is my shoe shop," said the man, "and the Lord has told me that I'm to give you a pair of shoes. So take your pick from all that you see here." Brian was completely amazed and dumbfounded and went home from that weekend with a brand new pair of shoes. As he said, "It taught me once and for all that the Lord is no man's debtor. Whatever we give God, He gives us far more back."

Figure 24 BCW Derwen Fawr Italian Garden in 1964.

Figure 25 Derwen Fawr Gardens 1964

Figure 26 The conference hall at Derwen Fawr 1964

Figure 27 BCW Derwen Fawr 1964. The rounded building back left was the
Chapel and the hut to the right contained two lecture rooms.

Figure 28 The vegetable garden behind the conference hall at Derwen Fawr

6. Together at Bible College

In 1965, at the end of Brian's first year at BCW, he returned home. Just before the end of the summer term Mr Samuel had told Brian that there was a place for Stella at the College the following year if she felt she should come. But the children's work that Stella had started in her home was going really well and she was committed to it and didn't feel that it was right to leave. She said she would only take the place at the Bible College if someone could be found to take her place with the children.

Once again the Lord made clear His plans for the couple. Within weeks, in July/August 1965, a well-documented polio epidemic affected Blackburn and as a result all school and children's meetings had to stop. Stella now felt that this was the Lord's answer and that she was at liberty to return to college with Brian. However, when he telephoned the College Brian was disappointed to discover that the place had been filled. It seemed that Stella wasn't meant to go to college after all and so a disappointed Brian returned alone to Swansea in September.

However, within a week of his return he was told that one of the female students had dropped out and with Mr Samuel's permission he immediately phoned Stella to ask her to join him as soon as she could. Ultimately she just missed one week of the term.

Even though they were married, Brian and Stella stayed in separate hostels and the rule was that male students did not fraternise with female students while in College. They managed to meet together occasionally for fellowship outside College, but for that year they lived as singles. Brian found it very hard, but Stella was strong and they lived by the rule.

This rule of the College would probably not be understood by most people either then or now, but they had both accepted that this was the life God had called them to while they were at College based on voluntary obedience to Paul's exhortation in 1 Corinthians 7:5, "Do not deprive one another except with consent for a time, that you may give yourselves to fasting and prayer" (Brian would add 'and to the word of God'). Brian says, "We knew it was right for that time and Father God honoured us for our obedience."

Figure 29 Brian and Stella – first year together at BCW

The second-year students were expected to share a room with a first-year student and the first thing that they did together was to share their testimonies together. Brian's room-mate in his second year was a Lancashire lad from Nelson in his early twenties called David. He had been born in Columbia and spoke fluent Spanish. His father had been a missionary with the Church of the Nazarene out in Columbia. His parents had now retired and returned to Britain and his father taught Spanish in night school in Nelson. Brian was reminded of his challenge to the Lord that if He really wanted him to go to Chile then he would meet someone who could teach him Spanish. God had confirmed His word and Brian realised that Chile was truly God's calling on his life. By one means or another he was sure that eventually he and Stella would serve the Lord in Chile.

David sent home for some Spanish text books and Brian began to learn. However, a short time later, David fell ill and was diagnosed with liver cancer. The disease was terminal and although he fully believed in divine healing he also knew in his spirit that the Lord was going to take him home. During the summer term of 1966 David died and Dr Symonds sent a group of students, including Brian, to Nelson to be bearers at his funeral. David never got to teach Brian Spanish. But Brian was still sure that Chile was somewhere in his future.

Figure 30 Lectures in the Italian garden with Ieuan Jones (back, standing) BCW Derwen Fawr

It is helpful to give some attention to the general church background at this time. In the wake of the Azusa Street Revival in Los Angeles from around 1906, the Pentecostal Revival had spread around the world. The British Pentecostal movements had their roots and flourished in the wake of the 1904 Revival in Wales. The Elim (1915 onwards), Assemblies of God (1924) and Apostolic (1909) movements were well supported and attended, particularly among the working classes. Prominent in these movements were Welsh Christians, many of whom had been converted in the 1904 Revival. In fact, both the Elim and Apostolic movements had their roots in Wales. However, the Pentecostal churches were viewed with much suspicion among the mainstream denominations and many Pentecostal believers suffered criticism and even ridicule for their faith.

In the 1960s a second wave of Pentecostalism, the charismatic renewal movement, was also spreading among many mainstream denominations, but not all. Because the College accepted students from all Christian denominations, including some who did not recognise the Baptism in the Holy Spirit as a separate experience from conversion, one of the conditions of enrolment was that students would voluntarily refrain from the use of spiritual gifts during College meetings. This was not because of any doctrinal objection by the College (quite the opposite actually as doctrinal studies at the College dealt with the teaching and endorsed it), but purely so as not to give offence to students from those denominations who were not persuaded by Pentecostal teaching. In fact, it is interesting to note that among the leaders of the charismatic renewal movement of the late 1960s onwards were graduates of the Bible College of Wales.

That said however, at this time there was a real thirst among many of the students for a richer and deeper spiritual life. Among the male students, Brian and a number of other students had experienced the Baptism in the Holy Spirit, and through praying together and sharing together, other men also experienced the blessing. This was not so much the case among the women, although many of them were seeking and praying for the experience. From the time that she had first read the story of Rees Howells and been prayed for at Caernarvon, Stella had continued to long for that blessing.

It was announced that Campbell McAlpine, a regular visiting speaker and a prominent figure in the charismatic renewal movement, would be coming to speak at the College. Brian recalls that the week before he came the men were particularly led to pray for the women students, asking that the prayers of many of the women who were seeking the baptism in the Holy Spirit would be answered. Unusually at that prayer meeting Brian recalls that one of the men gave a message in tongues which was then interpreted. Through that message the Lord assured them that He was going to bless the female students.

Campbell McAlpine spoke at each meeting from Friday evening until Sunday evening. Brian was unable to be there on the Sunday evening as he was speaking at a nearby church. This is Brian's account of what happened.

"After taking the evening meeting of one of the churches in Swansea, I went straight back to the College and went to the conference hall to find Stella. I just knew in my spirit that something had happened - there was such joy around the place. People were still being counselled in the back room at the conference hall but I could not find Stella anywhere and I was a little concerned because it was getting dark.

There was a place where we often met outside the College to share some time together. It was on a hill overlooking Swansea Bay just two streets away from the College. I decided to go there and when I got near I saw Stella sitting on a rock with her hands raised and worshipping the Lord in tongues. She was full of joy and worship. I was so delighted, I just enjoyed the time with her, thrilled that the Lord had filled her with His Spirit in answer to her prayers.

I asked her what had happened. She told me that Campbell McAlpine had spoken on Jesus raising Lazarus from the dead. When Jesus called him forth from the tomb he was still bound in the grave clothes in which he had been buried. He was alive but not yet free. Jesus commanded those present to loose him from the grave clothes and let him go. Campbell McAlpine likened this loosing to the Baptism in the Holy Spirit and offered to pray with any who were seeking that baptism. He then called people to come forward and prayed for them and offered counselling to anyone that needed it.

Many went forward, including Stella, who also went for counselling. He spoke into her life, then prayed for her and told her to go out and worship the Lord. She felt she needed to be alone and so went to the spot where she and I would often meet, and having begun to worship she began to flow in the Spirit and the gift of heavenly languages. She told me that she just felt so free to follow and to serve Her Saviour. From that day onwards Stella had such a passionate hunger for the word of God.

When we got back to College we noticed that Campbell McAlpine was still counselling people for the Baptism of the Spirit and that continued until early morning. There were so many that came through and most of them were the female students as the Lord had promised in our prayer meeting. For a number of days after, there was great joy around the College and an even greater desire for prayer and worship."

Figure 31 Female students - hostel cleaning party. Stella back left.

Early in the spring term of her first year in College, Stella received a letter from her stepmother Florrie to say that her widowed birth father Bill was travelling up north on a visit. He had been brought up in Preston and intended to visit a cousin who was a lock-keeper on one of the canals. Florrie also said that Bill was intending to visit her while he was in Lancashire. Shortly afterwards Stella received a second letter from Florrie saying that Bill had proposed to her and they were to be married around Easter.

However, when the time came neither Brian nor Stella had the money to travel home for the wedding. They prayed and asked that the Lord would provide. They were still praying and waiting on the Lord right up to the day before the wedding. Stella was extremely upset at the prospect of not going and sought the Lord with much weeping. They were now really torn as to what to do. They knew Stella's brother Johnnie was travelling up from Brighton and Stella really felt she should be there for Florrie who had been so kind to her. They thought about telling Mr Samuel about their dilemma but somehow felt that they shouldn't, even though they knew he would be sympathetic.

The only thing that Brian could think of was to ring his brother Roy and ask him to lend them the money. Roy had told Brian that if he was in need he only had to ask, but Brian had never asked and having learned to live by faith, he felt strongly that he shouldn't ask. But now, seeing Stella so upset, he decided that he would ask and so he rang his brother Roy and asked him if he could go to the station and book them a train ticket so that they could travel home. Roy agreed but found that it couldn't be done! The British Rail regulations wouldn't allow him to pay for a ticket in Blackburn - it had to be purchased in Swansea. Stella by this time had got to the point where she wanted to pawn her watch to raise the money for the fare home.

They knelt to pray together, Stella weeping and feeling desperate at their situation. They turned to the "Daily Light", a regularly used devotional booklet of selected Bible readings and found that through the reading for that day the Lord spoke to them powerfully. Matthew 10:37, "He that loves father or mother more than me is not worthy of me." This was a really difficult test to face. Stella wept and wept but finally said, "Father, if that is your will, your will be done."

Figure 32 Bill and Florrie's Wedding with Stella's brother, Johnnie

At the end of that term the couple faced a further test of faith when they realised that they had not got the money for their term fees. The College fees were not excessive but each student would undertake to pray and trust God for His provision to cover the fees at the end of each term as part of their commitment to a life of faith. If the end of term arrived and their fees hadn't been paid, then the student would voluntarily stay on in College until they had received provision to cover them. Brian particularly recalls that Dr Symonds' commitment to the men in his charge was such that he would not leave College himself for a holiday until the last of his students had "come through".

But they trusted that the Lord would provide and eventually the money came through. Brian and Stella had just enough time to return home for a short break before the end of the holidays. They travelled home, concerned that their absence from the wedding had upset Florrie and Bill, but were thankful and happy to find that they were understanding and not upset in the least. After a short period in Blackburn, they returned to College for the final term of the year.

Figure 33 Students cleaning at Sketty Isaf

Shortly after Bill and Florrie got married, they fell out. Bill left her and returned south to Brighton, and Florrie wrote to Stella to tell her that her dad had left her. Shortly after this, Florrie, who was diabetic, suffered a "hypo", and fell down some stairs. Neighbours wrote to Stella to tell her what had happened, but although it was against every natural instinct Stella felt the Lord was telling her not to go home. Again this caused her a great deal of anguish, although ultimately the situation worked out in an unexpected way.

Figure 34 Student cleaning party - Brian is 3rd from right.

At the end of that final term of the College year, Brian and Stella were preparing to go back to Blackburn. At the end of that term Stella had "come through" for her term fees but Brian had not, and so the both of them stayed on praying for God's provision. Brian had decided not to return for a third year, but Stella was anxious to get home because she was coming back for her second year in September and she needed the summer break. However, there was no sign of Brian coming through and so they agreed that if nothing changed by the following week, Stella would return to Blackburn alone and Brian would follow once his fees had come through.

It has already been mentioned, but it is worth repeating the principles regarding the basis of faith which was taught and lived out at the College. When something was needed, prayer would be continued until there was a breakthrough and a position of assurance was attained. This was the way in which the Holy Spirit taught and led Rees Howells and after him many others who learned to follow his example. This principle was applied to the smallest situation or need as well as the greatest crisis or situation involving national and international affairs. Having prayed to the point where the outcome was assured, even though the actual request had not yet been answered, prayer turned to praise while the outcome was patiently waited for. Once the position of assurance had been gained, then ultimately faith became substance and God provided – not necessarily in the way that the person who prayed envisaged that it would, but always the situation would be resolved.

Brian was reading a book by Andrew Murray entitled *The Blood of the Cross*, when God spoke to him through the book and he knew in his spirit that God was going to provide and that Stella wouldn't have to go back to Blackburn on her own. So confident was he that he told Stella that the Lord would provide the necessary funds on the following day. Sure enough a cheque arrived the following day for the exact amount that Brian needed and the two of them travelled home together to Blackburn for the summer. Another lesson of faith had been lived out and another reason given to praise God for His providence and faithfulness.

Their delayed return home also turned out to be providential in another way. Assuming that Brian and Stella were back in Addison Street for the summer holidays, Bill had travelled back up to Blackburn to retrieve some of his clothes from Florrie, intending to stay with them. He arrived in Blackburn suffering from a severe bout of flu, but found that the couple were not home. As a result he had no recourse but to go to Florrie's. She took pity on him and looked after him while he recovered. When Brian and Stella finally arrived home it was to find that Bill and Florrie had been reconciled – more cause for praise and worship!

Brian recalls that they arrived home on a Sunday with just a shilling (approximately 5p) in their pocket and practically no food in the house – just a little oil, a little flour and a little rice. Brian went out and bought an egg for sixpence and Stella made a sort of flatbread with the oil and flour, boiled the rice and they shared what they had between them. That evening they decided to go to the Elim church – a church that they hadn't been to previously. At the end of the service a collection was taken up and all that they had between them was the remaining sixpenny piece. So Brian put the last money they had in the collection. Brian remembers that somehow this just felt right after he had done it. As they were walking out, a lady came up to Brian and shook his hand and in her hand was a five pound note which she transferred to his and simply said, "God bless you." Yet more cause to bless the God who promises to "supply all your need according to His riches in glory by Christ Jesus" (Philippians 4:19).

7. A Year Apart 1966/67

The course at the Bible College of Wales was a two-year course with the option of a third year for those who were going into full-time service or ministry and at the end of that year in 1966, Brian did not feel that he wanted to stay on for the third year. He had always suffered with ear problems and his hearing wasn't good in spite of treatment from Dr Symonds who had been an ENT specialist. His poor hearing continued to cause him difficulties and so, after the summer of 1966, Stella returned on her own for what would be her second year.

Figure 35 Dr Kenneth Symonds lecturing on tropical medicine. Stella is behind on the right.

Brian remained in Blackburn, doing all sorts of building and plumbing work for his brother Roy, who by this time was buying and renovating older houses. Although he didn't realise it at the time, this was valuable experience for Brian – he got all sorts of practical experience which would stand him in good stead for later service. In addition he continued to work with Mrs Lamont doing practical work at the safe houses that she ran and also with M.O.V.E.

During that year at Blackburn, Dr Symonds of BCW contacted Brian and asked if he could fulfil a preaching appointment in Shrewsbury at Crowmoor Baptist Church. He explained that a student who had been due to go there from the College couldn't go. So Brian caught the train to Shrewsbury and arrived on the Saturday to stay with the pastor of the church. The pastor showed him to a bedroom and said that the bed might still be warm but it had clean sheets and that Dr Martyn Lloyd Jones had been speaking at the church the evening before and had left that morning. Brian was stunned! Here he was speaking at this large church where the Doctor, the minister of Westminster Chapel, London, and one of the most eminent preachers and leader of the time, had spoken on the Friday evening.

The following morning the church was packed and it was afterwards that Brian learned (although Dr Symonds had given no hint of it) that Brian was preaching there with a view to an appointment as an assistant pastor!

He spoke in the main church in the morning and then shared his testimony at a separate meeting at an outreach at a local school in the evening. He returned to Blackburn on the Monday and the following week received a letter saying that the church had unanimously agreed to call him as an assistant pastor. He knew he had to turn the offer down in the light of the Lord's call to Chile and also because of his continuing hearing difficulties.

However, he admits that this was a confusing time. He and Stella had written to every missionary society that was active in Chile offering their service in that country but they hadn't received one reply. Brian knew that CLC (Christian

Literature Crusade) had a work in Chile but he didn't want to apply to CLC because, being partially deaf, he didn't want shop work as he didn't think he could conversing with customers.

8. Together Again at College 1967/68

The following year in 1967, Brian was contemplating going back to BCW to complete a third year alongside Stella. The third year was optional and mainly geared to training men and women for church ministry as pastors or as missionaries. Unbeknown to Brian, Stella also felt that the Lord would have them both return for the third year together. When she came home for the summer break, Brian shared how he felt the Lord was leading him, and Stella was overjoyed. Brian immediately applied to College to see if they would accept him back to do a third year. He was successful and Mr Samuel agreed that the couple could have a room in Sketty Isaf (across the road from Derwen Fawr) on Saturdays, were they both could have time together. They were overjoyed with this news.

That summer vacation in Blackburn was a great time of relaxation and blessing for them, but also because Stella was able to spend time with her father and her stepmother.

The couple returned to the Bible College in 1967 and this proved to be one of the best years that they spent in College. Even though they lived as though they were single, they were together most days in morning lectures and spent time together on Saturdays.

They had continued to rent the terraced house in Addison Street, Blackburn, so that they would have somewhere to go to back home during the holidays. Over that period two female students from the College went to Blackburn from BCW at different times to work with Mrs Lamont and so Brian and Stella were able to let them have the use of the house rent free while they were there and when they wanted a break from the work. Brian still looks back on this period with amazement at God's provision for them even though there were times when they didn't know how they were going to pay the bills. But step by step every need was met.

Brian recalled that during this time they received a utility bill for either gas or electric at the rented house. They didn't have any money to meet the bill and Brian started getting final demand notices. He had no money and the only thought that occurred to him was that his brother Roy had said to him that if he needed anything desperately he could ring him for help. But it went against all that Brian had learned and so he committed the whole matter to the Lord in prayer and put his faith in the Lord, trusting Him to meet the need.

Then a letter came threatening a court action and Brian prayed again, now accepting that he might have to go to court and maybe face a fine or imprisonment, but in prayer he boldly reminded the Lord that it was His name that was at stake because Brian was determined to trust Him. Within days, a cheque to cover the debt arrived.

Figure 36 Rowland Evans, baker and intercessor with Christmas cakes

Another lesson and experience in living by faith and the Lord's provision came at the end of the first term of that third year in College. Again Brian and Stella had been waiting on the Lord to provide for their end-of-term fees, but they hadn't come through when the term finished a week before Christmas. Christmas drew ever closer and finally on Christmas Eve they both received the answer to their prayers. They had just enough money left then to get a bus back to Blackburn, but travelling on Christmas Eve was not going to be simple. The bus route was from Swansea to Birmingham Bullring and then they had to change to a London-Blackburn service. At Swansea they could only book as far as Birmingham because the operators couldn't guarantee any seats on the Birmingham to Blackburn leg of the journey. So they had no alternative but to trust the Lord and hope for a seat when they got to Birmingham.

Arriving in Birmingham they found the large bus station packed with travellers making their way home for Christmas. They had an hour before the London-Blackburn bus arrived, so they headed for the booking office. The news wasn't good. It wasn't possible to book seats on the coach and the booking clerk told them that their only chance was to queue for the coach and if there were any seats available they could book them through the driver. When they left the booking office they could see a long queue around a hundred yards away at the position where the coach would arrive. The prospects of getting home seemed hopeless. They started to make their way across to the queue when Brian heard the Lord saying that they should stay where they were, some 50 yards away from the queue, and trust Him and pray. Brian shared this with Stella who agreed. So they prayed, "Lord, You brought us this far, now we just trust You to take us the rest of the way."

After a little while they saw the London coach coming in, and again Brian heard the Lord saying that they should just stay where they were and trust Him. The coach pulled into the allotted bay and they saw the driver open the door and they saw a lot of people crowding around him. But he just shut the door and pushed his way through the queue and walked to the booking office. After a short time he came out of the booking office and walked back towards the bus, but then went out of his way to pass the spot where Brian and Stella were standing. To their amazement he stopped and asked them, "Where do you want to go?" Brian, a bit stunned, told him they were trying to get home to Blackburn. "Come with me," he said, and walked them back to his bus, taking them through the queue and onto the bus. He put them in the last two available seats on opposite sides of the aisle. They were just amazed and spent the journey rejoicing in God's provision for them in answer to their prayer. Yet another great step in proving God's faithfulness and living the life of faith.

After the Christmas period and at the beginning of the New Year in 1968, they arrived back at College to continue once again with their studies. The lectures were held in Sketty Isaf house in the sitting room that was used by the women students. It was a nice comfortable room and because there was only a small number of around ten third-year students that year, Brian found it a lot easier to hear, and was much more relaxed knowing that Stella was in the same room. The main lecturer was Ieuan Jones who was the principal lecturer in the College and a man whom Brian and Stella grew to love and regard as a spiritual father in Christ.

Figure 37 Stella, Elfie (Dutch) and Marlene in kitchen at Derwen Fawr.

Figure 38 Third-year Students at Sketty Isaf. Ieuan Jones on the left and Brian and Stella in the centre.

On most afternoons the third-year women students would go out to a local Swansea church where they were allocated to work alongside the pastor as a church worker. Stella was allocated to Ebenezer Baptist church in the centre of Swansea working alongside Pastor Leighton James.

This church had quite a long and illustrious history. Before becoming a Baptist church, it had been a Congregational church in the 19th century. One of the highlights of its history was the story of a young boy named Griffith John who lost both his parents at a young age, was accepted into membership of the church at the age of eight and ultimately trained to become a minister at the Congregational College at Brecon. He was ordained at Ebenezer and then within a few weeks he was married there. After his marriage he and his new wife spent their honeymoon on one of the tall ships sailing out to China.

They arrived out in Shanghai where they worked with Hudson Taylor, learned Mandarin and translated the Bible into a number of dialects. They were the first missionaries to move into the interior of China where they set up a hospital at Wuhan. Today that hospital is one of the main research hospitals in China and sees over 2,000 patients a day. He built a church of 32,000 members, only returning home twice in 52 years of service in China. He died in London on the 25th July, 1912, and is buried at Bethel Chapel, Sketty, which is just five minutes away from The Bible College. Stella was so blessed to be working at Ebenezer throughout her third year. It's also interesting that the story of Griffith John proved to be inspirational for Brian who continues to this day to take an interest in his story, and in recent years there has been greater acknowledgment of his dedication and influence in China from the Chinese people and local Swansea historians.

Figure 39 Norman Grubb, President of World Evangelisation Crusade (WEC) and author of *Rees Howells, Intercessor* with Mr Samuel Howells at BCW

Figure 40 Brian with Mr Geoffrey Crane, a teacher at the school, 1972, just before he left to teach in Israel

Figure 41 Pastor Arthur Lewis, lecturer in Bible Doctrine. An apostle in the Apostolic church and a powerful preacher and man of God. He and his wife lived in this caravan at BCW near the conference hall. He was much in demand as a conference speaker.

Figure 42 David Davies and Annie his wife who had served as missionaries in the Congo and had witnessed the powerful revival that took place there in 1953/54. They lived through the Simba uprising of 1964 and, on their return to Swansea, David taught at BCW for 26 years

There were only three male students in the third year, including Brian. The Bible College supplied a church called Salem in Morriston which was four miles away from College. The three students covered the church, taking it in turns to preach there as well as having other preaching engagements at other churches in Swansea and further afield. They did open-air work in Swansea and had permission to go into a local dance hall to witness amongst the young people. They also helped with first- and second-year students at the College, so all in all life was quite full in that year.

During the Easter break, Brian and Stella returned to Blackburn. During their time there they visited family members whom they had not seen for some time. Brian tells of a remarkable incident:

"When we arrived, the family were playing a children's game made by the well-known firm of Waddingtons. I asked about the name of the game and how it was played. It was called Ouija Mystifying Oracle - we had never heard of any such thing before. The board had an alphabet in two rows and a row of numbers from 1 to 10 with a 'Yes' and a 'No' and a 'Goodbye' panel. Two people were using the board while the family asked questions. The board then spelled out answers to the questions.

"We were amazed because it appeared that it seemed to be giving the right answers to the questions asked. Stella and I looked at each other and we both agreed and told the family that we felt that this was demonic. They disagreed, pointing out that it was just a children's game and argued that it would not be sold as such if there was anything harmful about it. Stella and I both felt we should leave, but then the Lord spoke to me and said, 'Don't leave, challenge them about this.' So I told the family that I would prove that the game was demonic. I said, 'Ask the board what I am thinking.' I was thinking about the precious blood of Christ. There was no answer from the board. So I said, 'Ask the board why it could not answer.' This time it answered, 'Because they are of God.' 'Now ask it what it thinks of Jesus.' The answer came in a single word, 'Bad.' 'Why is He bad?' The answer came, 'Because He is the Son of God.'

"By this time the family were fearful and wanted to stop, but I said that I had one last question, 'What is the one thing you fear?' The answer came, 'The Word of God.' The family immediately stopped, took it out to the yard and burned it. Hallelujah!

"Then one member of the family took us to a friend's house and they also had one of these games. We told them what had happened, but the friend argued that there must be good spirits as well as demonic and that there was no harm in using the game. The family member said, 'Prove it to them Brian'. I did not fancy going through all that again, but again the Lord prompted me to show them. The couple worked the board and asked, 'Are you a good or a bad spirit.' The answer came, 'A good spirit.' said The friend said, 'There, I told you so – there are good spirits.' I said, 'Ask him who he is.' They asked, 'Who are you?' And the answer came back, 'SATAN.' They broke the board in half and threw it to the floor. I thanked the Lord Jesus.

"What had happened sadly did not bring them to Christ. The Lord showed me later that He would not use the testimony of demons. It's significant that Jesus always told them to be quiet. But the family and friends did not forget what had happened that day. They realised that demonic forces are real and seek to deceive and lead many astray who open their minds to them."

Fairly soon after it had been released by Waddingtons, the BBC News announced that the game had been withdrawn from sale because of the bad effect it was having on children.

Figure 43 Rowland Evans in the bake-house at Derwen Fawr

8. Together Again at College 1967/68

Figure 44 Dan, an American student just returned from service in Vietnam, with an Indian and Nigerian student working in the Italian Garden at Derwen Fawr.

It has already been noted that Ieuan Jones, the principal lecturer at the College became a personal friend and spiritual father to Brian and Stella. They often visited Ieuan and his wife Sarah in their home. Brian was able to help Ieuan practically when he could. Once when the couple had what seemed to be an insoluble problem, they visited Ieuan to ask for counsel. He listened carefully and after some thought said, "Let us pray." His simple prayer made a lasting impression upon them both. He simply said, "Heavenly Father, they have come for bread, and I have no bread to give them." That was it! But the couple realised that here was a godly man who simply spoke the truth. Brian said, "That prayer never left us. Soon afterwards the Lord provided a solution to that problem, praise His Name. Later, Ieuan Jones would speak into our lives – words that would make a big impact and to mark a change of direction for us. He was a true spiritual father to us."

The College was blessed with lecturers and speakers who were not only excellent in their specific fields but who were also godly men who exercised a great influence for good on the students. Besides Ieuan Jones, the senior lecturer at the

College who with his wife Sarah had been former missionaries, Brian recalls Arthur Lewis who had an Apostolic church background and taught doctrine. With his wife he lived at the College in a caravan parked near the conference hall. The well-known pastor and evangelist, David Shepherd, came in to lecture on evangelism and also on the book of Hebrews. Then there was David Davies who had been born in nearby Gowerton. He had married his wife Annie in 1949 and had subsequently served the Lord in the Belgian Congo (now Zaire). They had witnessed a powerful revival during 1953/54 and by God's grace had survived the violent Simba uprisings of 1964, after which they returned home. David and Annie lived in a caravan on Gower and David lectured at the College for 26 years without pay. He was much in demand as a speaker. Brian recalls that he was particularly fond of the book of Jeremiah and he regularly spoke at Sunday services at the College when there was no visiting speaker. Dr Symonds, an ENT specialist who had devoted himself to the Lord's service at the College, lectured on all sorts of practical and tropical medicine. He was a great encourager and looked after the welfare of the male students at the College. Besides the regular staff, the College was blessed with many visiting speakers and lecturers. The staff members also comprised many men and women who served in practical ways as well as contributing to the spiritual and intercessory work of the College.

So Brian and Stella continued with their studies and their work with the local churches. It was a wonderful and profitable year for them both and they acknowledged God's faithfulness and His provision for them both.

After graduating, they left the Bible College and returned to Blackburn, still not knowing what God intended for their future, but confident that in due time He would reveal His will for their future service and help them to fulfil all that He had in store for them, but also confident that Chile was still in their future.

9. Blackburn and a Return to Swansea 1968/1973

Back in Blackburn in 1968 the future still seemed unclear. In spite of many applications to missionary societies, there were no opportunities for service in Chile, so while they were waiting on the Lord to show them the way forward, Brian went to work as a butcher working for a Blackburn meat processing firm and Stella, who had always been drawn to nursing but had no qualifications, went to work as an auxiliary in a Catholic hospital.

While she was working at the hospital one day she was surprised to see Bill Wilson, her dad. He had an appointment to see a consultant and subsequently it turned out the he was suffering from advanced bowel cancer. Stella was able to nurse him through his last days and to lead him to faith in the Lord Jesus Christ during this time. This came about when Stella asked him about his earlier wartime experience with the evangelist Gypsy Smith. He told her the story and when he got to the point where he recalled how he had responded, he broke down in tears and Stella gently led him to the Lord. Bill died in 1969.

The nuns at the hospital where she worked recognised Stella's nursing skills and urged her to go for training. With nothing opening up for Chile she prayed about it and felt strongly that State Registered Nurse training would be her next step. She applied to Blackburn Royal Infirmary and having no formal qualifications was required to sit an entrance exam which she failed. The hospital offered her the opportunity to train as a State Enrolled Nurse (SEN) but she was adamant that the Lord was calling her to train as an SRN. The Lancashire Evening Telegraph advertised a special jobs' supplement which was devoted to nursing training and positions, so Brian bought a copy. All the training adverts were for SEN training and they were disappointed until they spotted the only advert for SRN training - at Morriston Hospital near Swansea! They were amazed that a Welsh hospital was advertising in a Lancashire newspaper!

Stella wrote to the matron and was invited to go down for an interview and an examination. This time, Brian spent time helping Stella prepare for the exam and they went down to Swansea to stay with friends while Stella was at the hospital. Stella was accepted and so in 1970 they returned to Swansea to stay with friends until they could find their own accommodation. It turned out that Stella had to spend the first year of training in the nurses' accommodation at the hospital so the couple would be apart yet again. However, Brian visited the College and Mr Samuel Howells kindly offered him work and accommodation at the College during that year. At the end of the year the couple were able to share a room at the College for the remainder of Stella's training and for a further years' experience as a staff nurse.

Figure 45 Stella with the Morris 1100 car outside their room in College.

Brian worked as a handyman at the College for the four years. His brother had found them a small car, a Morris 1100, and Brian used it to take Mr Samuel to the bank and to do other business as required. He also took him to visit relatives and friends and got to know him very well.

One of the staff at the College, Tobias Bergin, who was known as Uncle Toby, was an excellent car mechanic. He taught both men and women students about car maintenance in order that they would be equipped for the mission field. A few of the students who showed an interest in car mechanics would be taken further and Uncle Toby taught them how to strip an engine down and put it back together again. The College had a well-equipped garage with a pit and Brian learned how to service his car and keep it in good order.

Figure 46 Uncle Toby

Uncle Toby was such a blessing to the students, always willing to lend them his own car when needed. His car was his pride and joy and yet never once did he refuse to lend it to a student so long as they put some petrol in the tank. Brian recalls that if anyone failed to do that they were likely to be told about it in no uncertain terms. Toby always regarded the car as the Lord's car.

9. Blackburn and a Return to Swansea 1968/1973

Brian recalls some adventures with the Morris 1100 that he owned. One summer's day a group decided to take the two cars, his and Uncle Toby's, on a trip up to the Black Mountains - a popular destination and an area where Rees and Samuel Howells had been born and raised.

While they were there Brian picked a piece of heather and stuck it in the grille at the front of the car. This was commonly done as a token of good luck. He recalls feeling a little disturbed at the time but shrugged off the feeling and left it there. At the end of the day out they set off to return to the College with Brian following Uncle Toby. Toby's car had a tow bar fitted to the back and as they were driving down the hillside a car shot in front of Toby who managed to pull up quickly. But Brian could not stop in time and ran into the back of Toby's car. The tow bar had hit the grille right where the heather was and pushed it through inside the grille.

The 1100 had a transverse engine and the radiator was actually mounted inside the nearside wing of the car and so was not damaged, but the tow bar had gone through the grille and smashed the distributor cap mounted on the front of the engine. The cap and its leads were the means of supplying the four cylinders with the electrical spark to run the engine and without it the car would not run. The man who had caused Uncle Toby to brake sharply surprised everyone by stopping, getting out of his car and apologising. He was driving a six-cylinder car.

When they inspected the damage to Brian's car they saw immediately that they would not get it going without a new cap. The man asked them to wait while he looked in the boot of his car. They were astonished when he came back with a distributor cap for a four-cylinder car engine, exactly what was needed. He gave it to them with his apologies. They fitted the cap and all was well. The curious thing was that the man had no reason to be carrying that cap because it would not be suitable for his car. So they continued on their way back to College and Brian was able to repair the damage to the grille.

Brian realised that he had been taught a lesson by the Lord. He had placed the heather on the grille for good luck but there is no such thing as luck or chance with the Lord who controls and provides all things. Recalling the incident, Brian said, "Father God is so gracious to us and merciful in the small things of life as well as big things."

Figure 47 Brian working on the wall at Derwen Fawr. The inward-facing panel read "Ebenezer - hitherto has the Lord helped us" while the outward panel read "Bible College of Wales. Have faith in God."

On another occasion Stella and Brian had to make an urgent trip home to Darwen. Leaving the College they needed to stop for petrol and having filled up they set off. Brian realised that he had not fastened his safety belt so he stopped the car and opened his door slightly to get hold of the belt. As he did so a large truck went speeding by. The rear bumper of the truck caught the door of the car and ripped it in two. The truck did not stop. Brian and Stella first gave thanks to the Lord that Brian was OK and then, realising that they were now in some difficulty, they prayed about what they should do and asked the Lord for help.

Brian knew that there was a scrapyard nearby with car parts for sale. So they headed for the yard. Their Morris 1100 was a dark green colour and to their astonishment when they went into the yard Brian saw a spare dark green door that was an exact match, but it had no lock. Brian bought the door and they headed for the Morris car dealers to see if they could buy a lock to fit. The dealers had one in stock but Brian realised that now they would have to carry an extra key just for the new lock which would be a nuisance. But having bought the lock and fitted it, they discovered that the key was identical to the key that fitted the other door lock and ignition. The chances of that being the case were remote . After three hours of work at the College the car had been fixed and they were once again on their way, praising the Lord for his goodness to them. Again Brian and Stella learned that in spite of the difficulties that came their way, the Lord's provision for them was perfect.

In 1972 Duncan Campbell came to BCW again and his subject was yet again about the necessity of putting everything on the altar. But this time he also emphasised that the offering is incomplete until the last piece is in place. Brian and Stella realised the Lord was speaking to them about holding on to the rented house and their furniture in Blackburn and that they had to trust Him for everything. As a result Brian went back to Blackburn and sold all their furniture and gave up the house.

Figure 48 At BCW, 1969. Stella (seated) now training for her SRN with BCW student cleaning party

It is worth pausing and reflecting on God's leading and provision for the couple at this point. As we have seen, the whole ethos of the Bible College of Wales and Rees Howells' example continued by his son Samuel, was one of absolute commitment and faith in God's provision for every aspect of life. The whole of Brian and Stella's lives up to this point and beyond were lived out on this principle. From the time that they sold all that they had in obedience to the call of God and for the rest of their lives together they looked to the Lord for leading and provision and their testimony was that the Lord never let them down. All through these long years of preparation for ministry God led and provided, often in unexpected ways, often at the very last possible moment, but His providence never failed. Note also the amazing answers to prayer over this period. From the moment that they committed themselves to sell up and follow the Lord's leading and guiding, His providence was evident often in the most remarkable way

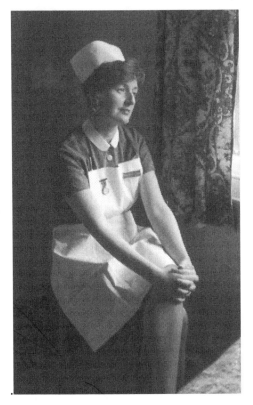

Figure 49 Stella Halliwell, SRN

Stella successfully qualified as a State Registered Nurse on the 29th March, 1973, and commenced working as a staff nurse at Morriston Hospital. Brian was still working at BCW but they both still had Chile on their hearts. Although there seemed little prospect of fulfilling the call that still seemed to be strong, neither of them could see how that call would be fulfilled.

Figure 50 Nigerian student carrying bread from bake-house, 1973

Figure 51 Derwen Fawr following repainting in the 1970s

That year Gwladys Thomas[8] spent some time at the College. Gwladys had taught at Emmanuel Grammar School but had left to pioneer, with others, a school at Ramallah, a

Palestinian city in the West Bank. She spoke to Brian and Stella and asked them to consider coming to Ramallah to be house parents to some of the children at the school. This was a very attractive prospect for Brian and Stella who had always wanted to visit Israel. They agreed, on condition that they could go for a year at a time because the call to Chile was still strong upon their lives. Gwladys Thomas agreed and that evening they walked along to Mumbles to telephone relatives in Darwen to tell them the news.

The prospect of going to Ramallah really seemed a wonderful opportunity and they were both excited about it. The telephone kiosk was near to Oystermouth Castle in Mumbles where they made the call and they started back for the College. Suddenly the lights came on at the top of the castle and illuminated a lady singing. Intrigued, they walked up to the castle to find out what was going on. They discovered that a pageant was being rehearsed called "The Bells of Santiago". It told the story of how four copper bells had been bought as scrap after a devastating fire at a church in Santiago, Chile in 1863 in which over 2,500 people died - one of the worse single fire tragedies in history. The bells had been bought by Graham Vivian whose family were involved in the copper industry in Swansea and the copper ore trade with Chile. Three of the bells were housed in All Saints' Church in Oystermouth where the Vivian family had a pew and the fourth one was given to St Thomas' church at Neath.[9]

Brian and Stella were completely taken aback as they listened and their excitement at the prospect of going to Ramallah completely faded away as they realised that this was the Lord's way of keeping them focused on Chile. They had to go to Miss Thomas and explain what had happened and that they couldn't go to Ramallah. She understood their decision and the Lord's calling on their lives.

Unbeknown to them, that very week events were transforming the situation in Chile. On the 11th September, 1973 the Marxist government of President Salvador Allende was overthrown by the newly-appointed commander in chief of the army, General Augusto Pinochet in a coup d'état. Allende died (later proved to be suicide) when the presidential palace was stormed. General Pinochet was to head up the military junta that ruled Chile until 1988. This transformed the situation for Christian agencies working in Chile. Aneurin (Nye) and Anne Williams had worked as missionaries in India and had joined Christian Literature Crusade (CLC) when it was the literature arm of WEC (Worldwide Evangelism Crusade). Nye was now on the CLC Finance and Personnel committees of CLC. He had spoken often with Brian at the College and knew about his call to Chile.

Figure 52 Ann and Nye (Aneurin) Williams

Just after the Chilean coup, Nye came to the College and gave Brian and Stella application forms and asked them to fill them in because a six-month candidates' course was starting in London within the next two weeks. In November 1973 Brian and Stella went up to London to CLC HQ for an interview, taking with them the completed applications. Brian confesses that he was quite taken aback and yet amazed at the way the Lord was leading them! He had solidly refused to consider CLC because of the shop work and worries about how he would cope with it because of his partial deafness. He had known that CLC had a local presence in Chile and now he was realising that this is what God had intended all along.

However, there were more hurdles to overcome. The CLC leadership had a very strict health policy and Brian and Stella had to undergo thorough medical examinations with a Harley Street specialist.

Brian was still suffering with his ears and at the time he had a severe infection in one ear which caused a continual discharge, and as a consequence he failed the medical. The overseas secretaries at CLC, Alistair and Hilary Cameron, stood firmly behind them at this time and Hilary got Brian an appointment to see a Christian ENT specialist. Brian prayed about the situation and the Lord told him to begin an open-ended fast.

He fasted and prayed for two weeks spending much time on his knees waiting before the Lord and after two weeks he knew that the fast was complete. He went to the appointment at St Thomas' Hospital in London and when the specialist examined him he found no infection in the ear at all. All he could see was a hole in Brian's eardrum and he said that a skin graft over the hole would help prevent any further infection and discharge in the future, but he could not guarantee an improvement in Brian's hearing. Within weeks the procedure had been carried out and a subsequent hearing test showed that his hearing in that ear was now just one point below normal – Brian could hear really well. So the application for a Chilean visa could go ahead.

Figure 53 Stella with Corrie Ten Boom at a book launch in the London CLC shop where the couple trained before leaving for Chile.

The local leader in Chile, who would be crucial in getting a visa approved, could not be contacted at this time because of all the turmoil in the aftermath of the coup. This threw much doubt on whether visas could be obtained.

But then a letter arrived from the Chilean leader. He had been invited by the Billy Graham organisation to the first Lausanne International Congress on World Evangelism in Switzerland and he was travelling via London.

Brian and Stella spent some time with him and an interpreter - he could speak no English and at this time they had little Spanish. They took him around London and he stayed at CLC headquarters.

Figure 54 Brian and Stella with the Chilean leader Rasmo Caro

While he was there on the following day Alistair Cameron telephoned the Chilean embassy to check on progress for Brian and Stella's visas, but was told that there was little chance of obtaining one in the current circumstances.

Unusually, Alistair was phoning, not from his office, but from a public telephone in the corridor. He seemed to be getting nowhere with the embassy when the Chilean leader walked past on his way to the kitchen. On an impulse Alistair grabbed his shoulder and handed him the telephone.

He spoke for some time with the embassy official in Spanish and after a time handed the telephone back to Alistair. The embassy official told Alistair that the visa could be granted but that Brian and Stella had to be in Chile within a month. It seemed that the Lord really wanted them in Chile.

9. Blackburn and a Return to Swansea 1968/1973

Figure 55 Stella in London with Chilean leader Rasmo Caro and an interpreter.

One final hurdle remained. They had to provide their own airfare. So CLC immediately put Brian and Stella on deputation work and as part of that they were sent to Sheffield. They were there about two weeks before their departure date when a further difficulty arose. Florrie, Stella's stepmother, was by this time in an old people's home in Blackburn and Brian and Stella received a telephone call to say that she had suffered a stroke and died. They immediately went to Blackburn for the funeral. Even though Stella was her next of kin, Florrie had left her estate to a neighbour but had bequeathed Stella £200. Stella could have contested the will but she felt strongly that it was not the right thing to do and was content to allow Florrie's will to stand. So two weeks later Brian and Stella arrived in Santiago Chile after a 26-hour flight via Brussels and Argentina with a suitcase each and £200.

Figure 56 Official CLC Photograph

10. First Mission to Chile -1974

Stella and Brian left for Chile in October 1974. On their arrival in Santiago they were met by the Chilean leader and an American missionary who did the interpreting for them. At that time they had very little Spanish. Normally they would have attended a language school before leaving for Chile but because the terms of their going were strict they only had a few weeks to enter the country. The plan was for them to find someone who could teach them the language when they arrived.

From the airport they were taken to visit the pastor of the Jotabeche Methodist Pentecostal Church[x] in the centre of Santiago.

Figure 57 Jotabeche Methodist Pentecostal Church, Santiago, Chile. At one time this was the largest Pentecostal assembly in the world with a membership of over 90,000.

The pastor's house was at the back of the church and after a meeting and sharing fellowship he asked them if they would like to see the new church that was about to be opened. They said that they would love to see it and so he took them down a corridor which actually led to the pulpit. They stood amazed at what they saw - the church would hold 12,000 people. It had a balcony for the musicians which would seat 200! It was so big and beautiful. The pastor said that he would send them an invitation to the opening.

Figure 58 Central and Southern Chile (© Google Maps)

When they left there they were feeling rather tired. After all they had just endured a flight of over 26 hours with stops, but there was to be no time for sleep for Brian. The leader told Brian that he wanted him to come with him on a mobile book mission in various places en route to Valdivia in southern Chile (approximately 530 miles away). He said that Stella could stay with his wife while they were away. The trip would take around two weeks! Brian agreed and asked when they would leave. To his great surprise the leader proposed leaving later that same afternoon after they had had a meal at his home! He asked Brian to pack a small case for himself and be ready to leave. So Stella stayed in Santiago with his wife, and Brian set off with the leader.

The van was already prepared with a load of books and Bibles for the trip down south. Brian felt so tired from the lack of sleep, but they set off and on the way they picked up a Christian couple who were travelling part of the way with them. They travelled for a few hours then stopped at a pastor's house where they were going to stay for the night. The pastor greeted them, took them into his house, gave them a lovely late evening meal and began to talk.

By this time Brian was feeling so tired he couldn't stay awake, so he motioned to them with his hands to indicate that he needed go to bed. They showed him to the bedroom which contained two three-foot single beds. Brian was soon asleep but was woken up later in the night when he became conscious of someone getting into bed beside him. To his surprise he realised it was the Chilean leader. The married couple who were travelling with them got into the other single bed in the room!

For Brian this was all a bit of a culture shock but he soon learned that this was quite normal in Chile and soon accepted that this was usual when they went on mobile trips around the country with the team. The following morning, they set off to visit other pastors and churches, and at one point the couple travelling with them arrived at their destination and left them.

Figure 59 Typical mobile display

Brian was very aware that the country was still on high alert, and as they were travelling and passing through each town there was a roadblock at the entrance to the town where soldiers were stationed and required identity cards to be shown before they would allow travellers to pass through. It was only nine months since the coup and a curfew was still being imposed at night.

One thing that the CLC Chilean leader had forgotten to tell Brian was that he needed to take his passport with him. So when they came to the first town and he asked Brian to pass him his passport to show the soldiers manning the road block, Brian had to tell him that he didn't have it with him. The soldiers were quite strict and threatening, and Brian, not being able to communicate properly with them, was obviously intimidated. However, they let him pass through. Thanks to the Lord's protection and provision Brian did not once get asked for his passport again during the rest of their two-week trip although his companion had to present his identity card every time. Even today Brian looks back upon that trip with amazement at God's grace in keeping them safe and enabling them to pass around the country without hindrance. He remembers enjoying visiting the churches, meeting the pastors and witnessing and praising God for the amount of Bibles and Christian books being distributed.

Figure 60 Mobile book display

Another highlight of the trip was visiting Valdivia. There was a volcano nearby at Villarrica that had only recently stopped erupting and was still smouldering. The pastor who they were staying with wanted to take them part way up the volcano. So they set off that morning and as they drove the truck up towards the volcano, the landscape looked as though an atomic bomb had exploded. All the trees were stripped and burnt so that they looked like dead matchsticks. The ground was still very warm as they drove over it and there was a strong smell of sulphur in the air. It was an experience that Brian said he would never forget. They went about a third way up the volcano and then turned round and came back home. He heard after that they should not have made that trip - the volcano was still in a very active state.

They came back to Santiago having travelled hundreds of miles, visited many churches and distributed many Bibles and books during the two-week trip. For Brian it was a great start to their ministry in Chile although he wished that Stella could have been with him.

Figure 61 Sleeping rough where they could on mobile mission

The following morning the CLC leader took them to the place where they would be living. It was in an upper class part of Santiago. When they arrived at the property they found that it was a bungalow which was rented to the lady who had interpreted for them when they first arrived in Chile. She already had another lady missionary from England staying with her and so there was no room to stay in the bungalow itself. She took them into the back garden and showed them what appeared to be a small washhouse. It was damp and just contained a three-foot-six bed, and a stove on which to cook! That little outhouse became their home for a few months. The next important thing was to learn the language so they were taken to a lady teacher to be taught Spanish in her home.

After a few months they looked into finding a house of their own. They found a two-bedroom bungalow situated in the middle class Las Recas area of Santiago among the

Chilean people and this became their home till the end of their first stay in Chile.

The CLC leader took them to meet the team at the bookstore and office which was in the centre of Santiago. First they met Mary who was his secretary and was bilingual. Then they were introduced to Achilles, the accountant who spoke a little English, and a married couple named Eduardo and Alysia, who only had a few words of English. All of these became their close friends.

As the weeks went on the team learned that the CLC mission was not in a good shape and had debts of over 20,000 dollars. It also seemed that the relationship between the team and the leader was not good. Brian and Stella found themselves distracted by these problems at the time when they should have been concentrating on learning Spanish. They felt bound to raise the issues with the responsible international field office that CLC Chile was under, which was located in North America. The international leader made several trips to Chile and after a few months the Chilean leader left his post leaving the work without leadership.

The team then looked to Brian and Stella to take them forward. Mary became their bilingual secretary. Her command of English was excellent, having been brought up by an American father and having a Chilean mother. From that point their need of the language teacher grew less and less as they started to pick up the language with Mary's help. Brian and Stella were the only team members able to drive and that meant that they had to do many mobile trips down to the south of Chile with Eduardo and Alysia. Gradually, through a lot of hard work and after many tiring trips, the mission began to be able to pay off the debts that were owing to the publishers.

In September 1975 the pastor of the Jotabeche Methodist Pentecostal Church invited Brian and Stella to the opening of the new building as he had promised them on their first day in Chile. This was also a thanksgiving service held by the evangelical churches of Chile on the anniversary of the coup d'état which had ousted the Marxist government of Allende two years previously. The churches invited the members of the military junta to attend and they accepted.

Figure 62 General Pinochet attending Jotabeche Church in 1975

On 14th September, 1975, Stella and Brian were shown to the front of the 12,000-seater church and were seated in front of the pulpit just to the left, facing the congregation. On the front row of the congregation facing the pulpit and them was the president of Chile, General Augusto Pinochet. Brian recalls, "We did notice him looking over at us. He was probably wondering who these foreigners were - although I must say that the Chilean people are very pro-British." After the meeting they found themselves being interviewed by the radio station. This celebration became a regular event each year and Brian and Stella were often invited to attend, but not with the same privilege of sitting at the front!

When they had arrived in Chile, there were three CLC shops. Two were in arcades - one in Santiago, another in

Concepción and the third shop was in Valparaiso connected to a church building. CLC had only obtained the shop in Valparaiso a few weeks before they arrived in Chile but due to the financial circumstances, they realised that they had to close it. Brian was saddened by this but the Lord spoke to him as he prayed about the situation and promised him that one day he would once again open a shop in Valparaiso. CLC England gave them £200 and with that they refitted the Santiago arcade shop. They built shelves all around the walls and made it look like a proper bookstore.

The need for indigenous Chilean leadership was still on their hearts. A Chilean couple were running the bookstore in Concepción and the team felt at that time that they were well suited for the work of leadership. When asked, they accepted but did not want to move from Concepción being happy to carry out the leadership role from there. CLC agreed and from that point on things began to flourish. CLC Chile was offered the distribution rights for Editorial Vida publications for Chile which they accepted. Later on many more publishers also gave them distribution rights.

As time went on it became apparent that they needed a bigger bookstore with warehouse facilities. Brian presented this need to North America where the founder of CLC, Ken Adams, lived. Ken contacted them and offered Chile a $20,000 interest-free loan. They were overjoyed and grateful for the offer which was duly accepted.

Ken had visited Chile and stayed with Brian and Stella during one of his trips. He saw the work that they had done and one evening in their home he gave them a prophetic word. Through it God showed them that their work and ministry was to be finding and fitting out new bookstores in all the places where He would show them.

Figure 63 Ken Adams with the Chilean Team

The team began to look for a suitable property around Santiago but because inflation was very high and property was the safest investment at that time, no one wanted to sell. It seemed an impossible task. It was also around this time that the national currency changed from escudos to pesos.

The Bible Society was moving out of their premises and they offered to sell it to CLC. The shop was a little outside of the shopping centre but it did have a large warehouse. At the time nothing else could be found and the team felt that there was no other solution but to purchase the Bible Society property.

On the day that they were about to sign Stella and Brian felt led to take a walk around the centre of Santiago. They came across a large shop right opposite the telephone tower which had only just been put up for sale. The owner was Argentinian and was due to arrive in Chile wanting a quick sale. They immediately brought the team to view the premises and found it to be just right. The sales floor was 126 square metres and had a basement area of the same size for the wholesale department. It had one other major benefit, the added blessing of a lift, something that was quite unusual to find in a building in Santiago. There were no problems in the negotiation. The Argentinian accepted their offer of $20,000. The timing of the Lord was so perfect and so gave the team more cause for rejoicing and praise!

Figure 64 Santiago

Brian began designing the bookshelves with the help of Stella and then with the team they fitted out the bookstore. On 26th March, 1977, about 100 people gathered for the dedication service. It was such a wonderful time. It was one of the largest CLC bookstores in South America.

Figure 65 Santiago shop basement, storage and goods lift.

Around that time there was a disagreement between Brian and the international office regarding the leadership in Chile. The international office felt it needed to be changed. Brian's health at the time was not great and because of that and the dispute, the international office decided that Brian and Stella should return to Britain.

Brian and Stella sought the Lord together and individually about their future in Chile. They both had the same strong conviction that they should stay in Chile. They shared this with the mission in Britain, but the mission insisted that they had to come home. They found this decision hard to understand and at first they both felt that they should stay, even if it went against the wishes of the British international office.

But as they continued to pray the Lord challenged them, asking them, "Where is the Cross in all of this?" They realised that the answer was that they were called to lay everything down at the foot of the Cross and to submit to those that the Lord had placed in authority over them. And so that is what they did. Having accepted the mission's decision, the Lord spoke to them again and said, "You will come back to Chile one day. Meanwhile, rest in Me". So on the 2nd April, 1977 Brian and Stella left Santiago and returned to London.

11. Back to Britain 1977

Back in Britain, the CLC Missionary conference was held in the month of May 1977 and there Brian and Stella were to meet with the personnel committee to discuss their future. In one of the conference meetings the need of a manager for the Southampton shop was brought up. Sitting behind Brian and Stella was their leader Les. He tapped them on the shoulder and said, "How about you both taking it on?" Somehow this seemed to strike them both in their spirit as the way forward. So they accepted the challenge.

On arriving at Southampton and settling in, they took over the management of the shop. They made a few changes in the presentation and the shop flourished under their care and under the Lord's good hand. The shop sales increased each year and they both thoroughly enjoyed their time there. In 1978 they moved into a ground floor flat in Cambridge Street, Southampton.

They got involved in a charismatic church which then joined up with another church. It came to be known as the Southampton Community Fellowship, It grew to become quite a large church having two pastors. The church was under the overall care of Arthur Wallis, the well-known Bible teacher, leader and writer, who was like an apostolic covering for them. As well as running the shop they also took on the leadership of a house group from the church. Their time there was a fruitful and happy one.

Brian now takes up the story himself. "After a few years of being in Southampton and the Lord using us to help many people in a pastoral way, the church asked us if we would like to go up to Andover and begin a fellowship there. There was a small house group there who had made this request.

"I always wanted to have the opportunity of pastoring a church. But this meant that we would have to leave the CLC mission in order to move to Andover. We then began to look to the Lord and pray about what we should do. At a meeting we attended, Arthur Wallis spoke about Peter stepping out of the boat and walking on the water. We felt that the Lord was speaking to us through that word. In 1982 we left CLC and went to live in Andover for nearly two years. The work there began to grow. We rented a bungalow and a community hall, established the work there and made many great and precious friendships.

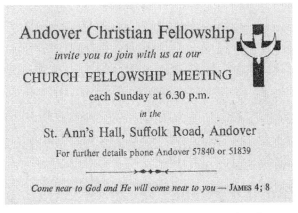

Andover Christian Fellowship

invite you to join with us at our

CHURCH FELLOWSHIP MEETING

each Sunday at 6.30 p.m.

in the

St. Ann's Hall, Suffolk Road, Andover

For further details phone Andover 57840 or 51839

Come near to God and He will come near to you — JAMES 4; 8

"Then problems began to arise with other leaders outside of Andover. Stella and I began seeking the Lord's will for us in this situation. We thought again about how we had felt led to go to Andover in the first place, recalling again the way the Lord had spoken to us through the account of Peter stepping out of the boat in obedience to the Lord in Matthew 14: 24-34.

"We had understood at the time that the boat represented the mission that we were in and that in obedience we too should step out in faith, leaving CLC and be obedient to the Lord's calling to Andover. But now as we prayed about it the Lord began to show us that although Peter stepped out of the boat and began to walk towards the Lord, in the end the Lord took Peter by the hand and they went back to the boat together. It occurred to us that now the Lord might want to take us back into CLC. We prayed and waited, looking to the Lord.

"A few days later Ieuan Jones, the principal lecturer at the Bible College of Wales and a personal friend and spiritual father to us, arrived unexpectedly on our doorstep. He had been visiting his son and he came to see us so that he could share something that the Lord had placed on his heart. He told us that he felt that the Lord wanted to tell us that His will for us was to be back in the CLC Mission. This was an amazing confirmation of what God had been speaking to us about. So at that point we reapplied to CLC and were accepted back on condition that we would spend three months in London to readjust to the mission. We willingly agreed.

Figure 66 Stella with Sarah and Ieuan Jones at Llanelli, August 1981

"In 1984 there was a need for a manager in the Leicester bookshop and we took this on. The work in Leicester was growing and eventually the shop became too small. We asked CLC if they would allow us to look for larger premises. We found a shop that had two floors above the ground floor. When they gave us permission, we fitted the whole place out.

Figure 67 Leicester Shop Exterior

Figure 68 Leicester - meeting room on first floor

"The bookstore was on the ground floor and on the first floor we had a meeting room that could seat 50, and the second floor became a store area. The bookshop was much larger than the original one and was nearer to the centre of the city. From there, the work began to grow even more.

Figure 69 At the Leicester shop in 1978

In 1987 the international office of CLC approached us and told us that they had appointed a new leader in Chile. The new leader was Pedro Pradenas, a Chilean who was an accountant. They asked us if we would we be prepared to go back to Chile again. It turned out that the international leader who had wanted us to leave Chile seven years previously was now asking us if we would like to go back. Father God was fulfilling His Word to us - that one day we would return to Chile.

"This proposition was put to the British field. They accepted with the condition that we went to the language school in Madrid in Spain for six months first. So in 1988 Stella and I went off to Spain to a Baptist language school in Madrid. We were there for the whole six months, having a great time and also being able to help CLC at a Gypsy Christian conference. It was wonderful seeing boxes of Bibles going out."

Figure 70 Madrid Language School

Figure 71 Madrid Gipsy Christian Conference

Figure 72 Just before they returned to Chile in 1989 Brian and Stella visited Nora Miller, a CLC veteran who had been a staunch prayer partner for Brian and Stella while they were in Chile

12. Second Mission to Chile -1989

On 22nd February, 1989, Brian and Stella flew off to Chile for the second time. On arriving in Santiago, five of the Chilean CLC team were at the airport to meet them, and from the outset they felt at home. After a few days of adjustment, they met with the leader Pedro Pradenas and his team to discuss present and future plans for their stay in Chile.

Figure 73 Northern Chile (© Google Maps)

The leadership wanted them to spend time in Concepción, Santiago and then go up north to Antofagasta to spend time with a senior member of CLC, Gladys Parada. She had moved there, to establish a book room in her home. During the six months following her arrival she had built up 20 church book deposits in the area but was unable to find a suitable premises for a shop.

Antofagasta is a city with a population of over 200,000. It is surrounded by the Atacama Desert, and has a coastline on the Pacific Ocean. It is one of Chile's major ports and is also important as a port for landlocked Bolivia.

Figure 74 Antofagasta

The Atacama Desert is the second largest desert in the world and known to be the driest. Copper and mineral mining plays a major part in that area.

Brian accompanied Pedro on the 18-hour coach journey from Santiago to Antofagasta to understand the situation for themselves and to search for a suitable premises for a shop. Within four days they had found a property in a central location, signed the contract and had the keys in their hands! They experienced God's guidance and provision in every way.

Returning to Santiago a few weeks later, Brian and Stella travelled up to Antofagasta to live with Gladys and also to plan, fit out and set up the shop ready for the inauguration.

Figure 75 Antofagasta Shop

Everything was completed within a month with just one last small panic which is worth mentioning! Two days before the planned opening ceremony, the official papers allowing them to sell books had not come through. One of team went to the government office to obtain them and was told that the officials did not attend to those particular papers on a Friday and that he should go back on the following Monday.

Feeling discouraged, they got together to pray and ask the Lord what to do. They felt that they should return to the office that same day and try again. There at the same office they spoke to another man, who, on hearing the story immediately went and obtained all the necessary papers and handed them over! They returned to the shop thanking and praising God.

On Saturday, 5th August, 1989 around 100 people gathered with them to dedicate the Antofagasta bookshop to the Lord's service. They were delighted and encouraged to see TV North filming the event and rejoiced while watching the item on the 9 o'clock news that evening. Brian testifies that

Antofagasta and the people of the Atacama Desert occupied a very special place deep in their hearts.

Figure 76 Antofagasta Shop Dedication

Brian and Stella then returned to Santiago where they rented a house and began their next assignment which was to find a second store to rent on the outskirts of Santiago, in the upper middle class area. This they did, first finding the premises, making the fittings, fitting it out and getting it up and running with the Chilean team.

Brian recalls, "It was wonderful to see so much happening and seeing the Gospel and the Word of God getting out through the printed page from our bookstores. We would often hear of people finding Jesus as their Lord and Saviour through the bookshops. Projects kept coming one after another. Stella and I felt that we were truly in the centre of God's will. The beauty of it all was that we were able to do the work a lot more cheaply than any contractors by keeping the costs down and doing all the work ourselves."

With more publishers wanting to give CLC the distribution rights for the whole of Chile, it meant that they needed a larger warehouse because the basement of the Santiago store had now become too small. The team had been looking on the outskirts of Santiago and found and purchased an old building near to the railway and the coach stations - the two places from which they distributed most of their boxes throughout the country. It was a great location and a good size, but the building at the rear was falling down.

Figure 77 Santiago warehouse frontage before building work commenced.

Brian said, "This project took a little longer because of having to get contractors in to make the building safe. My part was planning it all, plastering and decorating, making and setting up the fittings and also helping to lay it out." Brian was putting all the skills (and some new ones) to good use - skills that he had picked up in his younger days working with his father in Darwen and later with his brother Roy as they renovated older houses.

Figure 78 The rear of the warehouse building, Santiago

It gave Brian and Stella a great thrill to see the work completed in the warehouse and to see it up and running. At that time CLC Britain gave them a gift of money which enabled them to purchase two vans, one for the North and one for the south of Chile for mobile ministry.

Figure 79 The renovated warehouse

Figure 80 Santiago warehouse interior

Their final assignment for this time in Chile was to find a new bookstore in Concepción. The small existing bookstore was in an arcade between two larger men's outfitters shops owned by a man who had trained at Harrods in London! He had bought all the shops within the arcade and was anxious to purchase the bookshop. This made it easier for Brian to negotiate a good deal - if he could find another more suitable location for the bookshop in the centre of Concepción.

Figure 81 Concepción: the original arcade shop

Brian did find one which was a lot bigger but realised that the asking price was more than he thought the owner of the men's outfitters was prepared to pay for the arcade shop. Brian talked to him and soon realised that if he could persuade him to negotiate to buy the larger property on CLC's behalf, as a local he might well be able to buy it at a lower price. In fact he managed to buy it at a price which was equivalent to the price he was willing to pay CLC for the arcade bookshop.

Figure 82 Concepción: The new two-storey shop

So CLC got an amazing deal and the team thanked God for His provision and goodness to them.

Once the new shop was available, Brian and Stella made all the fittings and fitted out the new bookshop within about a month. They then had the joy of attending the inauguration and seeing the shop up and running.

Early in this second mission to Chile, Brian recruited a young Chilean Christian, Juanito, to help him with some of the shop fitting work. He was a cleaner in the Santiago shop but Brian saw his potential and helped him learn a number of practical skills. He accompanied Brian to Concepción while Stella remained in Santiago.

Figure 83 Juanito assembling bookcases at Concepción

At Christmas, Juanito invited Brian and Stella home for a meal with his family which they were happy to accept. They discovered that the family lived in a shanty town area of Santiago in very poor conditions. They shared a meal with Juanito, his wife Lydia and their five children. They had just a simple bed and a bunk bed for the whole family. The house had no running water or toilet facilities.

Figure 84 Juanito, Lydia and family - Christmas lunch

Figure 85 Juanito's House

Figure 86 Juanito and Lydia's home

Lydia became ill and was in a great deal of pain suffering with gall stones. She needed an operation but the family was very poor. Brian and Stella arranged and paid for her to have the operation and then Stella nursed her back to health in a spare room at their Santiago flat while Juanito took care of the children.

Figure 87 Lydia recovering from the operation at Brian and Stella's flat in Santiago with some of her children.

This kindness was repaid a short time later when Stella contracted paratyphoid while Brian was away from home. Lydia took care of Stella who became severely dehydrated. Lydia managed to contact Brian who immediately returned to Santiago. He took Stella to the German hospital where she was placed on a drip. At the end of the day she felt better and was discharged; before she left the hospital she became ill and delirious so she had to remain in hospital for a few more days, but recovered well.

Brian and Stella had a visit from one of the elders of the Countesthorpe Church near Leicester which they had attended before this second mission to Chile. Brian took him to visit Juanito and Lydia whose home was now under real threat of demolition. The elder was moved to help and with contributions from the church and from Brian and Stella £5,000 was raised towards the purchase of a small government-built house costing £5,500. The house was on an estate very close to the shanty town so that the family could remain close to their spiritual friends and neighbours. Brian arranged it so that Juanito could pay the remaining £500 by instalments. Brian and Stella obtained beds for the family and for the first time in their lives the children had their own beds.

Figure 88 Juanito at the family's new home

When Brian and Stella left Chile at the end of their second visit, they left all of their furniture with the family.

Juanito learned such a lot working with Brian that when CLC had to let him go he was able to work for himself as a handyman and successfully ran a small business and prospered.

On their return in 1996, Brian and Stella were pleased to find that the family were doing well and that Juanito was pastoring a small church at a hut that had been constructed in the neighbourhood of the shanty town in which he had formerly lived. It was encouraging to see how God had blessed the family.

Figure 89 Juanito outside the small church near his previous home.

Figure 90 The interior of the small church.

The Chilean government was stable during this time headed up by President Augusto Pinochet who was a controversial figure but sympathetic to the Christian church and missions in Chile. It was rumoured by many pastors that he came to know the Lord through a South American evangelist. What follows is part of the account of the CLC leader's meeting with the President.

12. Second Mission to Chile -1989

"In 1989 our CLC leader in Chile, Pedro Pradenas, was invited along with Mr Bob Hoskins, President of Editorial Vida publishers USA, and two Chilean pastors, to be present at a personal interview with General Pinochet, President of the Republic of Chile. The purpose of the visit was to present Bibles and to get permission to distribute *The Book of Life*, an account of the life of our Lord Jesus Christ, in the schools and colleges of Chile.

"We were received by the President, who was smiling and dressed in civilian clothes. The atmosphere was relaxed and informal. As we gave him a copy of the Bible he said, 'I have the Bible that Pastor Uribe gave to me and I am not like those who have the Bible, but do not read it. I have it and I read it every day, The Bible is important to me...' The conversation with the President took longer than anticipated due to the interest shown to us. 'Where is the bookshop of the CLC?' he asked, taking a piece of paper to write down the address. I gave him my card and said, 'We are neighbours, Mr President; the bookshop is at 57 Amunategui Street, just a block from here.' He responded, 'I may come to visit you. I like to read a lot.' We talked much about things of God and he responded by promising to do all he could to collaborate in the work of the Lord. Wishing him God's blessing, and with a strong abrazo (hug), we left the man who had been President of the country for 16 years.

"The week after the visit, CLC received a phone call from the President's secretary at the Palace requesting catalogues of our books. This was duly sent and shortly afterwards CLC received an order to the value of approximately $500 worth of excellent Christian books. A short time later a second order was placed for the same amount of $500. At that time we were waiting for certain titles that he requested which had not yet come in and so were holding the order until they arrived. The President's secretary once again rang, asked for the books and could we please take the books over that we already had, as the President was in bed with a heavy cold and would like them to read, which we did. We understand that among the gifts he makes to his friends, the President included Bibles and Christian books." Stella and Brian were in Santiago at the time and helped in putting the orders up.

The final meeting that Brian and Stella had with the team before they returned home was to discuss a vision to send a couple to the north of Chile to develop a mobile ministry with one of the vans that had been donated by the British field. They felt that this was a time to put this into action. The aim was to work from Antofagasta providing a mobile service to the Atacama Desert which covered an area of 140,000 square miles with a population of over two-and-a-half million living in scattered townships. However, it was now time for Brian and Stella to come home once again to Britain and they left Chile in 1991.

13. Back in Britain 1991

On their return they heard that the CLC bookstore in Swansea needed a manager so they wrote to the mission and offered to take it on. They were accepted. They enjoyed renewing their friendships in the area and settled to the work in Swansea, first renting a house in Cockett and then in 1992 a second-floor flat in Tycoch. At this time they felt that their time abroad had come to an end and that Swansea would be where they would stay until they retired. Little did they know what Father God was planning for them!

Figure 91 A day out on Gower enjoying the fine weather.

In 1993 they had a visit from the international representative for South America, who was Uruguayan. He had come to Britain to attend an international meeting of leaders of all the countries where CLC had missions. He asked if he could come to visit them in Swansea for a few days. While he was with them he told them what was happening in Chile. Among other things was the news that the project of setting up a mobile work in the Atacama Desert had been shelved. Brian and Stella felt sad about that.

Brian tells of what followed. "The following day we took our friend out down to the Gower peninsula to meet two other CLC workers who were caravanning there. On arriving at their caravan site we found that they had another young visitor who was a student at Swansea University. While Stella and I were on our own with the student we told her that we had been students in the Bible College of Wales and then had worked in Chile. The student then asked us whether we were Brian and Stella. When we told her that we were, she told us that she was the granddaughter of Ieuan and Sarah Jones. We knew that Ieuan had passed away just a few months before and told her how sorry we had been to hear of his death.

"We shared with her that her grandfather had been like a spiritual father to us both. She said, 'I have something to tell you, which my grandmother and I could not understand. When my grandad was very ill one day he called for my grandmother and said, *Sarah, the man from Chile is in the garden.* My grandmother did not understand what he meant and eventually left the room. Once again he shouted for my grandmother and when she came to him, he said again, *The man from Chile is in the garden.* My grandmother and I could not understand what he was talking about. Do you understand it? Maybe it's significant for you? I'll just leave it with you.' We were puzzled and could not give her an answer at that moment, so after a time of fellowship we headed home. On our way back I shared what she had told us with the Uruguayan leader. He too was puzzled as to what it could mean.

"By this time we had put Chile completely out of our minds. As far as we knew, we thought that the work there had come to an end for us. Deep down we did not want to go back. We were happy and content to remain in the ministry at Swansea until the day we would retire.

"The following day while resting in the bath and meditating upon what Ieuan Jones' daughter had told us, I seemed to feel within my heart that somehow this was a prophetic word from him. So I began thinking about the work in Chile, especially the one project that did not get going in the Atacama Desert. Knowing that there are no coincidences with the Lord, I could not help wondering whether these two things might be linked together.

"I began asking Father God what it all could mean. 'Lord why did Ieuan say, *The man from Chile*, when he knew my name?' The answer came. 'I have not finished with you in Chile. It will not leave you.' My second question was 'What's the meaning of *is in the garden*?. What's the significance of that?' The answer came in one simple word, 'Gethsemane'. I just wept and wept and I could not stop until I said, 'Not my will Lord, but Thy Will be done.' When I shared this with Stella, she wept with me. She did not even question it but just received it as a word from the Lord. It seemed that the Lord was telling us that we had to go back to Chile?

"We shared it with the South American international leader who was staying with us. He was interested in what we said, but non-committal. He just said that we needed to follow it through. We realised that our permanent residence visas for Chile had expired because we had been out of the country for more than two years. However, we wrote to the Chilean embassy anyway to see if there was any possibility that the visas could be renewed. We felt that if it were possible then that would be a confirmation that the Lord wanted us to go back. The letter came back from the Chilean embassy telling us that because they had expired they could not be renewed. I must confess that we felt very discouraged - by this time the call to go back seemed to be so strong.

"A few weeks later the British CLC field asked us if we would go to Newcastle to sort out a number of problems that they had there. They told us that they had a couple who could take over the management of the Swansea bookshop so that we could be released. We went up to Newcastle to see what the city was like and accepted the challenge. So in 1995 we moved to Newcastle. We enjoyed our time there, refitted part of the shop and turned the sales around. We also found a good church and enjoyed our fellowship there.

"But the Lord still kept reminding us about Chile. One day I felt the Lord was saying that I should write again to the Chilean embassy. This went on for a couple of days. I shared it with Stella and she agreed. We wrote off again sending off our old permanent visas, hoping almost against hope that they would renew them.

"To our amazement we received a reply saying that they would renew them but gave us a short time limit in which to return to the country. We thanked the Lord, Who by this time had also given us a real longing to go back to serve Him there.

"We then sent a letter to the leadership in Chile, telling them that we felt the Lord was calling us to open up a new work in a different town in the Atacama Desert. They replied that they would like us back, but first of all they wanted to reopen the work in Valparaiso before moving further north.

"When we heard about Valparaiso we were reminded that it was there that we had to close the shop on our first visit to Chile in 1974. The Lord had said to us at the time, 'One day you will reopen it.' We were only too glad to say yes to going back to fulfil the Lord's promise to us.

"Stella and I had trained up a young lady called Pauline, to take over the management of the shop in Newcastle. She drove us to the airport with God's blessing."

14. Third Mission to Chile - 1996

So on 9th April, 1996, Stella and Brian returned to Chile for the third time. Once again they were met by some of the Chilean team at the airport. After a few days' acclimatisation they met again with the team to discuss present and future plans for them.

The first project was to open the shop in Valparaiso in southern Chile, the main seaport and the second largest city in the country. They stayed in Santiago for nine days and then left taking three coach journeys of one-and-three-quarter hours each to get to Valparaiso. There they eventually found a flat which they could rent until the end of the year in Vina del Mar, a seaside town adjacent to Valparaiso. They settled into the flat and found this period a useful time in which to adjust back into the language and the culture. Brian recalled their time there:

"We were offered a small shop at the side of the Baptist Church which was in the city centre. We were not all that happy about the size, so with one of the team we searched high and low but could not find anything suitable. Then the Lord began to speak to us through the scriptures in 2 Corinthians 9: 8 'And God *is* able to make all grace abound toward you, that you, always having all sufficiency in all things, may have an abundance for every good work.' It speaks not only about having sufficiency in all things, but also in abundance for every good work. Well, the Lord gave us the shop, twice the size that we were wanting and at half the price, and in a more central position in accordance with His word. That was Father God's abundance!

"During the ten weeks of making up the bookshelves and fitting out the shop, the Lord protected us and gave wisdom and ability. On one occasion I remember we were invaded by bugs from the shop basement which took a liking to our little flat and our English blood! After spraying the shop and flat again and again we finally got rid of them!

Figure 92 Valparaiso - work in progress

"The Lord really blessed us on the day of the inauguration. Around 100 people turned up, mostly pastors and leaders of the region, plus Christian TV and radio. The day was finished off with a CLC Christian concert with a well-known singer from Mexico. The church was packed out.

Figure 93 Valparaiso - finished bookshop

"It was wonderful to see Father God answering our prayers and honouring His word that once again He would open a bookshop in Valparaiso. It was exactly 20 years ago since we had to close the bookstore during our first period in Chile. Now the first part of our new mission was completed! The Valparaiso CLC shop was open and going well with two Chilean workers continuing to be responsible for it."

Brian and Stella were now invited to travel to the north to attend a seventh anniversary celebration of the Antofagasta bookshop which they had set up on their second mission to Chile. Over 200 people were present at the meeting including many pastors. Brian recalls, "It was thrilling to meet up with the team of three working there and see how the work had progressed. This gave us an even greater sense of urgency to see the literature ministry extended to the far north of Chile."

While they were in Antofagasta they took the opportunity to visit Iquique, which was a six-hour journey north by coach. During three days there, they visited ten pastors and spoke to them of their vision, and all were very positive in their response. Iquique is the capital of that region and was a fast-growing coastal city of 170,000. It served as a main port for Chile and also for its land-locked neighbour Bolivia.

On their return south to Valparaiso they received a phone call from one of the leaders in Santiago to tell them that one of the pastors they had met in Iquique wanted them to know that he had a house available to rent there.

Pedro the Chilean leader and Brian flew up to Iquique (a two-hour journey by plane instead of 26 hours by coach!) to have a look. However, the house was not suitable for the needs of the ministry that CLC had envisioned. The need was for a house with a garage and a store room. Pedro and Brian stayed on for three days and for the first two days nothing seemed to open up.

When Brian phoned Stella she was disappointed that the house they had gone up to see was not suitable. But her Bible reading for that day was Luke 22:12. This is the passage where Jesus sends His disciples into Jerusalem to find a room where they might prepare the Passover meal. He told them that they would meet and follow a man carrying a pitcher of water and ask the master of the house that he went to, "Where is the guest room where I may eat the Passover with My disciples?" It was the verse following that stood out for Stella. "Then he will show you a large, furnished upper room; there make ready." She shared this with Brian. The following day Pedro and Brian went to see another house. It had accommodation on the upper floor and was fully furnished but importantly it also had a large garage and storeroom underneath the flat. This was a double blessing and just what was required. That same day the contract was signed! Brian says, "We praised the Lord for His provision and goodness. As you might guess we called our new home "The Upper Room".

Figure 94 Iquique (before)

On 5th November, 1996, Brian and Stella set off for Iquique. When they arrived they first went around visiting the churches and pastors and introduced themselves. Then they began the work to convert the garage below the house into a bookshop. The transformation was amazing and so were the number of people that started coming.

Figure 95 Iquique - the Upper Room

Brian writes, "To give you some impression of the area: Iquique is one of the driest parts of the world, it hardly ever rains! In our time there, the water supply was rationed, being cut off from 2pm to 7pm each day. The reason for this is that the water has to be piped a great distance from the Andes Mountains and has to be carefully rationed. The climate is called the eternal spring, yet inland the temperature goes from 35° in the daytime down to freezing point at night.

"The area in the north that the Bible shop would cover is the size of England! Because it is so large and mostly desert, the people are drawn together in scattered, isolated towns. For example, one town that we served was called Calama, which has a population of around 90,000 people as well as having the world's largest opencast copper mine situated at a very high altitude of about 3,000 metres. When the CLC shop was up and running in Iquique we had two students studying in Iquique who went home to Calama at the weekends, taking with them $500 worth of Bibles and books from the shop each month. Never once did I know them return any books. They were always sold!"

Figure 96 Iquique CLC finished.

Brian and Stella were in Iquique for almost a year. Then the CLC team leader asked them if they would take time off to go to Talca, south of Santiago, to convert a house there into a bookstore. They had a single worker available called Claudio who was about to get married and he would be sent to run the bookstore in Iquique while they were away.

They flew down to Santiago and then took a coach south to Talca. On arrival at the house they met the owners - a missionary couple who were in their eighties and were about to retire to Canada. The house was beautiful and in the centre of town, and at the back of the house in the garden was a wooden shed which opened onto a main street. The couple used it as a small Christian bookshop which they wanted to see continue, so they offered it and the house to the CLC mission at a cheap price. The leaders purchased the property, their aim being to transfer the bookshop into the house and to make a flat above it.

Figure 97 Talca (before).

Brian could see that this was going to be a big job. A lot of structural changes would have to be made. Walls would have to be removed and windows made larger - and this in a country that is prone to frequent earthquake tremors! They found a builder who was willing to come and work alongside them and help them through the difficult parts of the project.

Brian takes up the story: "And so in 1997 we went to live in Talca and started to work. It wasn't easy living above the shop and working down below. I had to cover the whole kitchen area with plastic sheeting to keep the dust out.

Figure 98 Talca - Stella in the kitchen

"After a week there the missionary couple who had lived in the house for more than 40 years commented, 'You are doing an excellent job of destroying our house!' Nine weeks later the same couple were invited to cut the ribbon at the inauguration for the new CLC bookshop.

Figure 99 Talca - the completed CLC bookshop.

"At the inauguration the husband joked, 'Be careful about inviting the Halliwells into your house. They might convert it into a bookshop!' It took a little longer than expected but it was a thrill to open up in December with over 80 people at the inauguration service."

At the bottom of the garden there was a wooden garage and it was in there that Stella and Brian were able to make the fittings for the shop. They were then asked if they could make bookshelves and set up a CLC exhibition in Santiago's International Book Fair which attracted 150 exhibitors. CLC was to be the only Christian evangelical exhibition stand. So once again they accepted the challenge. Brian recalls the success of the exhibition, "We really praised the Lord for this opportunity. Over £4,000 worth of literature was sold to mostly non-Christians as well as much free literature distributed."

Figure 100 The Santiago Book Fair Exhibition Stand

They travelled back north and arrived in Iquique a few days before Christmas where they found that Claudio had done an excellent job running the bookstore in their absence. The Christmas rush was on and the shop was open from 10am to 10pm then. The only day off they had was Christmas Day. But the Lord was blessing their efforts and Brian recalls, "We thanked the Lord that out of our 12 months in Iquique, December saw the largest amount of literature and Bibles going out."

Claudio returned to his home city of Concepción to get married in February. Then he and his wife Lorraine returned to Iquique in March to live in the flat over the shop and take over its running full time.

At this time in the mission many other projects were being proposed. One of them was a complete refit of the bookstore in Santiago that had been purchased when Brian and Stella first came to Chile. The plan was to enlarge it by making it into a bookshop on two floors now that they had a warehouse nearby. That meant converting the basement into a second sales floor.

In addition the international office of CLC asked the Chilean team if they would like to take on the project of opening a bookstore in Lima in Peru. Finally they also wanted the Antofagasta bookstore refitted as they had an opportunity to purchase new and larger premises. Stella and Brian were then 60 years of age and beginning to find the challenges a bit daunting.

They continued to live in Talca in a little wooden flat built above the garage. This brought its own problems. The garage was home to a lot of red-spotted spiders which were known to be poisonous. So inside the garage Brian covered all the walls and ceiling with plastic sheeting. He recalls, "Inside the plastic sheeting was my domain and the other side was for the spiders!" In the garage they made all the shelving and fittings for the Santiago shop - without once being bitten!

Brian then began travelling back and fore between Talca and Santiago, sometimes alone and sometimes with Stella. In Santiago Brian was working with and supervising workmen in the refit of the Santiago bookstore. It was a six-hour drive between the two places, and between travelling and work Brian found it hard going.

Near the end of their stay in Chile they were again invited to the annual Methodist Pentecostal Church celebration at Jotabeche. General Pinochet had stepped down as President in 1990 and the new democratic government had been in charge since that time. A new president had just been elected. Brian recalls:

"I had been working early in the morning refitting the shop and then we went off to the church celebration. We sat at the back of the church because we didn't feel as though we were properly dressed for the occasion. One of the church leaders came straight to us and asked us to follow him. He took us down to the front of the church and showed us to seats just three rows behind the President and amongst the cabinet members of the government! It so reminded me of that scripture in Luke 14 when the Lord said, 'But when you are invited, go and sit down in the lowest place, so that when he who invited you comes he may say to you, *Friend, go up higher*. This great church always respected us for our work in Chile."

In October, 1998, the former president of Chile, General Augusto Pinochet, went to the UK for medical treatment. Spain issued an extradition request that he should be sent to Spain to face charges of human rights' violations. He was placed under house arrest in Britain pending legal hearings and appeals.

The Chilean people had always been very pro-British but this action caused much confusion among them. Brian and Stella were constantly approached by the Chileans who could not understand why Britain had done this, especially after Chile had not only stood by Britain but had helped her during the Falklands War. Brian recalls that this was a very difficult time for them.

In spite of the many difficulties, they were able to complete the work in Santiago. It was hard going but ultimately it provided a vital resource for the 4.5 million people who lived in Santiago. The shop which now had two sales floors had been completely refitted and also a new goods lift installed. From the time of its reopening the Santiago shop flourished. The increased stock space attracted increasing numbers of the public. Brian and Stella praised the Lord and were thankful for His goodness to them and for giving them the strength and skills to see the project through.

Figure 101 Santiago refit complete

Before any further work was undertaken Brian and Stella were able to take a one week holiday in Iquique. They were delighted to see how well the work was going on there in the two years since it began. They also met up with Patricio, the manager of the Antofagasta shop (eight hours south of Iquique by bus), who was also in charge of the mobile work in the north, visiting the isolated towns in the Atacama Desert. They were thrilled to learn that the mobile effort had resulted in over £2,000 worth of literature going out each month - more reasons to praise the Lord.

At the CLC Chile conference the decision had been made to advance into Lima, the capital of Peru. A couple were lined up to go with Brian and Stella to establish and run the shop. Elvis, who was Peruvian and his Chilean wife Cecilia, worked as part of the CLC Chilean team in the Santiago shop and they both had a lot of experience in the warehouse and with imports. They had a four-year-old boy called Ricardo. It was estimated that the project could take between four and six months and would involve finding premises, fitting out the bookshop and getting the work up and running. At the end of that time it was planned that Brian and Stella would return to Chile while Elvis and the family would stay in Lima to carry on the work.

In order to get things under way, Pedro Padrenas, Elvis and Brian flew to Lima. There they met with the Bible Society accountant who briefed them on local and national procedures and they also visited the offices which dealt with imports. They then had fellowship with various pastors who were pleased to hear that CLC was planning to come to Lima to open a bookshop.

They also visited churches. One church they visited seated 750 and they had now grown to 4,000 members and had six teaching meetings of an hour-and-a-half each Sunday morning, the first one starting at 7.30am. The changeover from one meeting to the next was so efficient and quick that Brian was amazed to note that when one meeting ended and the next meeting started, the sense of God's presence just continued from one meeting to the next. The last meeting started at 4pm, then at 6.30pm an evangelistic meeting began. They witnessed eight people accepting Christ Jesus as their Savour in that meeting. From the little that they saw they sensed that God was doing a great work there.

They returned to Chile and Elvis and his family went to Lima ahead of them to find a flat to rent. On 16th October, 1998, Brian and Stella followed them. They began to look for a property to rent and Brian recalls: "Within a matter of days

God gave us what we had asked for and the owner dropped the rent to what we could afford!

"In just over three months the shop was opened to the public on 19th January, 1999. I had the privilege of serving the first customer. She asked me if we had a copy of *Rees Howells, Intercessor* by Norman Grubb. I was delighted to be able to tell her that Stella and I had trained at the Bible College of Wales and shared something of our story with her."

The inauguration of the bookshop was held later, on 27th March 1999. The Chilean leaders had planned for speakers and publishers to come and so they needed to give those who were invited time to make travel arrangements. The inauguration would include a breakfast conference to present CLC and the publishers to around 500 invited pastors and leaders. Brian and Stella were unable to attend the inauguration because at that time they were back in Chile and had begun the work of refitting a newly-located CLC shop in Antofagasta. Those who were in Lima for the inauguration reported it was a great time of blessing and thanksgiving.

Figure 102 Lima CLC Peru

Brian writes, "We were so blessed in being able to complete the work in the Atacama Desert. On 8th April, 1999 we had completed over three years on this third mission in Chile and Peru. During that time we had changed accommodation ten times. We had travelled thousands of miles. We saw four new shops opened and two bookstores refitted. We had managed the Iquique bookstore for a year. We had used over 1,200 square metres of laminated chipboard, putting on over 3,000 meters of edging and screwed in over 14,000 screws. This had taken its toll and we were both exhausted and needed a time of rest. At this point the Lord told us that it was time for a break."

Figure 103 Stella at Antofagasta

They returned to Santiago and then went on a holiday down to Puerto Montt in the south of Chile for two weeks and stayed in a log cabin situated on the side of a beautiful lake.

Figure 104 Puerto Montt

Brian writes, "The view from the balcony was stunning! Across the lake in the distance was a beautiful snow-capped volcano. We both felt so blessed by the Lord and praised Him for giving us the strength and His enabling to accomplish His work. It brought back to us the scripture that Father God had given us at the beginning, the story of Jesus sending out the seventy in Luke 10:1, 'Jesus appointed them and He sent them where He Himself was about to go.' He appointed Stella and me and He sent us out to a place where He had already gone before us. We were just so overjoyed and felt so privileged to have fulfilled His will through our lives and with His enabling. I look back with thankfulness and a sense of awe at all He did through us and with grateful thanks that He had blessed me with such a willing and loving wife, friend and partner, my beloved Stella. To our beloved Lord Jesus Christ be all the Glory."

Figure 105 With the Chilean team just before Brian and Stella left Chile for the final time

15. Retirement 1999

On 29th May, 1999, Brian and Stella came home from Chile when CLC mission decided that they should retire. They returned to Swansea where they settled down in a rented house in Pastoral Way, found for them by Parklands Evangelical Church.

Figure 106 Photograph taken just after Brian and Stella retired.

During the first few months of retirement Brian found himself having problems with an irregular heartbeat and was admitted to Singleton hospital. This proved to be the result of exhaustion from the work in Chile and Peru, but now, given time to recover, things gradually came back to normal and Brian soon got back to feeling well.

After six months the couple moved to a flat in Harford Court, Sketty, Swansea, near to the Bible College of Wales where once again they offered their services to help in whatever way they could. There was little that they could do at that time other than visiting and helping, and sharing fellowship with the older staff members which they did willingly.

During this period they also shared hospitality with a number of university students. Brian recalls, "Everywhere we lived Stella would open our home. In Chile we often had local children coming around regularly. While we were at Iquique there was an earthquake which destroyed a bridge on the main pan-American highway to the south. A group of tourists were stranded at Iquique and Stella arranged for two ladies to stay with us until the way south was reopened.

"Stella always attracted children wherever we went. Not being blessed with any of our own it seemed that Stella became a real blessing to the poorest and neediest children wherever we lived in Chile.

Figure 107 Chilean children who lived in the neighbourhood of the Iquique shop.

"The story was the same wherever we lived. In Leicester we got to know about a young Chilean man who had arrived in Britain just before Christmas and had nowhere to stay. He spent Christmas with us and Stella went out of her way to make him welcome.

Figure 108 Stella with the Chilean student who spent Christmas with us at Leicester

"In Swansea we helped a Chinese family who were from Xian where the terracotta army was found. The husband was at Swansea University and they were not well off. Stella gave her sewing machine to the wife so that she could make clothes for her children. At the end of their time in Swansea they took the machine back to China.

Figure 109 The Chinese Family at Swansea.

"Stella was the most generous and open-hearted person and we regularly entertained Christian and non-Christian students and others."

In 2004 Mr Samuel Howells the director of the Bible College died. In that same year CLC decided to close the bookshop in Swansea.

Figure 110 Swansea CLC Bookshop just before it closed with Nye Williams (seated), Moff and Gordon Oldham, who had managed the shop, and Brian Watkins who is still active with Book Aid.

Brian and Stella were asked if they would decommission the store. At the same time the Evangelical Movement of Wales (EMW) approached CLC to see if they could purchase the fittings from the bookshop. This was agreed and Brian offered himself to help in any way he could in dismantling and reassembling the fittings. Out of that came the work of fitting out a new EMW bookstore in Wrexham, North Wales.

Figure 111 Wrexham EMW bookshop.

Then, with the remainder of the fittings, Brian and Stella refitted the EMW Swansea market stall. This then led on to further work for EMW in Bangor, North Wales, and following that, with Stella's help, a shop at the EMW Theological College at Bridgend, and finally the market stall in Neath. Stella particularly enjoyed refitting Neath as it was the place where her biological mother Evelyn had been born. It gave her the feeling that she had done something for her.

Figure 112 Brian at Bryntirion Theological College (WEST) Bridgend.

Figure 113 Stella at Exeter Bookshop - their final project together.

At the end of this time Stella was beginning to show signs of difficulty with her memory. The last Christian bookstore they worked on together was for some friends in Exeter. Being in a strange town that they did not know well, Brian noticed that Stella was finding it difficult to find her way around, which meant that she could not be left on her own.

In 2006, Stella was diagnosed with Alzheimer's disease. As her condition worsened and she needed more attention, Brian had to spend more and more time with her. She began to have difficulty in finding her way around the block of flats they lived in. This meant that Brian had to consider moving once more. The answer seemed to be a move into sheltered accommodation where there was a warden on hand. At that time the only place where Stella felt comfortable going out on her own was in Mumbles, just down the road from Sketty. She used to visit an elderly friend who lived in sheltered accommodation in Mumbles and she told Brian that she would like to live there - somewhere familiar where she would feel secure.

They sent in the application forms for a flat but received a reply which informed them that there was a long waiting list. This was quite understandable as Mumbles is a popular and lovely place to live. They had their names down on the waiting list for over a year and then they received a letter which told them that their chances of a place were unlikely because they didn't have enough "housing points". The letter also asked them if they would like to choose to live in a different part of Swansea where there were vacancies.

Brian explained this to Stella but she was adamant that they keep their names on the list for Mumbles because she was convinced that God wanted them there. Around two weeks later they received a letter from a firm called Coastal Housing asking whether they wanted to remain on the housing list. This was confusing as they had not heard of Coastal Housing, but when they contacted them they found out that it was a housing association that had taken over the running of the flats at Mumbles.

A friend who lived in the flats rang to tell them that number 22, a ground floor flat, was about to become vacant. Stella was very excited and urged Brian to contact them. Brian prayed about it, looking to the Lord to know what best to do. He felt that he should go and have a word with their doctor who was sympathetic and gave Brian a letter explaining Stella's illness and needs. Brian took the letter to the letting office but the letting officer was sick; so he spoke with a young man, gave him the doctor's note and left. Brian and Stella prayed and committed the outcome to the Lord.

The following day the young man rang and asked whether they would like to view the flat In Mumbles. Stella wanted to take it immediately without a viewing, but the young man explained that they had to go to view it first. So they went down, saw it and immediately accepted it. Brian recalls that Stella had never lost faith that God would give them one of the flats at Mumbles. On 17th December, 2008, just before Christmas, the couple moved in with the help of the church. What a Christmas present the Lord God had given them. The flat was situated in a quiet area of Mumbles with the Medical Centre just around the corner, a three-minute walk to the sea front and ten minutes to the shops. It was just what they needed.

Moving to sheltered accommodation made life so much easier for both of them. Stella found it very difficult to accept that she had Alzheimer's and often tried to cover it up by saying that she'd always had a bad memory. She would pray that the Lord would take her home first before Brian because she knew that if Brian died first she would have to go into care as they didn't have any close relatives. Brian recalls that even though she knew that her condition was gradually growing worse, she never complained or questioned God's love and wisdom through this time of gradual decline. She did lose the memory of her time as a nurse and also as a missionary in Chile, but she never forgot that Jesus Christ was her Saviour and that whatever she was going through God loved her and would be with her at all times.

As the months and years went by, Brian had to take on more and more responsibility in caring for Stella. He began to realise how much work running a home involves! Washing, cleaning and making the meals took up most of his days as well as having to help Stella to undress and dress herself each day. Life for him became a constant caring for Stella which he patiently and willingly did as it meant that they could continue to be together. Their love for each other was as strong as it always had been.

One morning Brian recalls waking up feeling exhausted and wondering where God was in all of this. He suddenly felt very much alone. As he thought on this, with Stella still sleeping at his side, he heard the Lord telling him to get up and go down to the seafront. It was just before dawn, but he got up, dressed and went out. As he was walking down the street the sun was beginning to rise. He walked down onto the beach until the water was at his feet. Then from the sun came a shaft of light across the sea to his feet. In that moment it felt like God was saying, "Here I am; you have my full attention." Brian just started to cry. Then the Lord said to him, "Walk along the beach", and as he walked along he noticed that the shaft of light from the sun never left him and when he turned around and walked back the shaft was always there and the Lord said to him, "I have never left you, I am with you always, wherever you are, 1 am there." Such a sense of God's presence and relief came into Brian's soul that day and the weight of the burden was lifted and the sense of loneliness was gone (hence the significance of Brian's photograph of sunrise over Swansea Bay on the cover of this book).

Stella loved to go walking along the Gower coast. So most days they went for walks whenever the weather permitted, and Mumbles was the ideal place to be with walks so easily accessible.

16. A Heavenly Experience 2012

On a weekend in April 2012 Brian felt very ill. It was difficult for Stella to understand what was happening. On the Monday afternoon the weather was good and Stella wanted to go for a walk, but Brian was still feeling poorly. In spite of that he took her out, they came home, had their evening meal and went to bed.

This is how Brian described what followed:

"Around 9.15 on that Monday night, not being able to sleep and feeling so unwell, I thought I was about to pass out. I cried out, 'Stella, I've got to call for an ambulance.' We had an emergency pull-cord in the flat which I pulled and when the warden answered, I shouted, 'Get me an ambulance please.' I struggled to get Stella dressed and then laid down on the bed. The warden came and the ambulance arrived at 9.40pm. By then I was feeling a little better, but after some tests the paramedics rang my doctor who advised them to take me to hospital.

"A Christian friend, John, and his wife came and took charge of Stella. They followed the ambulance to Morriston Hospital in their car while Stella came with me in the ambulance. My concern was Stella and how she would manage. I started feeling very ill again. I could hear the bell going on the ambulance. On arrival at the hospital they rushed me into A & E and put me onto a bed. I thought that I was going to die and at first I felt fearful. This was a real test of my faith. The only thing I could think of doing was to pray in tongues to the Lord. It was then I began losing consciousness and passed out.

"Then I remember that the heavenly language I was speaking became completely intelligible and I found myself in a most beautiful place which is so hard to describe - it was so, so beautiful. The sky was a lovely light blue. I just knew that I'd come home and that it was all over for me on earth. It was so real and all fear had gone. Oh, how can I describe the feeling of joy and the reality of our heavenly home? I had such a strong impression that I had come from a battlefield which was raging on the earth and I had no desire to go back. As I turned to the left, I saw Jesus standing beside me. I talked with Him but I do not know for how long. This I do know - at the end of my time talking with Jesus, my last words were, 'I know Stella is safe with You and You will bring her home.' Jesus then swung His right arm over my head and with a powerful voice said, 'Go back and tell them, I AM ALIVE.' Then I felt myself returning to earth.

"As Paul said in his second epistle to the Corinthians when he described his heavenly vision, 'Whether I was in the body or out of the body, I do not know.' But this I do know, like Paul, I, Brian Halliwell, had been in the heavenly realms with Jesus Christ my Lord.

"When I came around, I saw John, my Christian friend, at the end of the bed. I sat up and shouted 'John, I've just been with Jesus.' He began to cry. Then I fell back and went out as though I was asleep. The next time I became fully conscious was on Tuesday afternoon when I came around in a bed that the hospital had found for me in the stroke ward.

"A few weeks later I saw my friend John, who had been in the hospital with his wife and Stella for four-and-a-half hours on the night I had been taken ill. I asked him how long I had been unconscious. John answered with his eyes filling up, 'I couldn't tell you Brian.' I somehow felt the Lord Jesus did not want me to know, but His commission to me was simply, 'Go back and tell them, I am alive.'

"When I regained consciousness in the stroke ward I found I could not speak. I had also lost my memory but not the memory of being with Jesus although I was unable to tell anyone. My eyesight was also affected in a most peculiar way. I saw numbers and letters all over the ward, like graffiti or like a computer screen that's gone wrong. It did not worry me because I had such a peace in my heart and was just able to rest in Jesus. Thanks to the Lord the stroke did not leave me without movement down my left side as is common. The peace that I felt remained with me right through my twelve days in hospital.

"After the first two days my speech started to come back. My memory took a few days longer but gradually it returned. It was good to be able to remember things like my PIN numbers and passwords once again. As for my eyes returning to normal, they took longer. When I first tried to read my Bible, I found the letters going off the page to the left - as I went along the line they all disappeared before I could read the words - this was very strange.

"I wasn't fearful or worried of what was happening but just continued to trust and rest in the Lord Jesus. I recall asking the Lord, 'How can I overcome this?' Amazingly the Lord said to me, 'Turn your Bible clockwise a quarter of a turn.' This meant that I was reading from top to bottom and not left to right, but from right to left. It was then that I found I could read the first line of my reading before it disappeared. I began memorising each line! During the days that I was in hospital I asked the Lord how to get back to normal reading again. He again said to me, 'Now move your Bible little by little anticlockwise.' Before the end of my stay in hospital I was able to read once again in the normal way. Thank you Lord, you knew what I had to do. At the end of my twelve days in hospital and having a few tests to see whether I could manage at home, they finally let me go out of hospital. I spent two days at home on my own before bringing Stella back to the flat.

"During my time in hospital, Stella had been put into a care home by Social Services. The home was a mixture of elderly people and one or two of them were suffering with dementia. This was not an ideal place for her and when I did eventually get her home I noticed that she had deteriorated a lot. We gradually got back to some normality. I have to say it was lovely having her back home again.

"When I made my first follow-up visit to see the stroke specialist afterwards, his first words to me were, 'You have made an incredible recovery and I could sign you off today but I will arrange for you to have an appointment to have another brain scan. If there is any difference, I will let you know.' All was well and I was seen by the stroke nurses for 26 weeks, which was the usual routine after suffering a stroke. Praise the Lord, He is so good and as Stella would always add, 'All the time'."

17. Stella's Call to Glory

Brian continues, "We then had just about a year together at home - going out walking most days. Then there came another downward step in Stella's condition. It seemed to me following the initial decline that nothing came gradually with the Alzheimer's - just sudden changes and always for the worse. Now Stella was waking up at 3.00am and wanting to go out and have a walk. She couldn't understand that it was the middle of the night, but neither could she get back to sleep. Ten seconds later she would then repeat herself. This went on until in the end I had to get up with her. The only thing I could do at that time of the morning was to take her in the car to the 24-hour Tesco store in Swansea to do a little shopping and then bring her back home. This went on for quite a number of days. Eventually I became more and more exhausted and had to call the doctor. She prescribed other tablets for Stella but nothing seemed to work. The doctor came again and said that the next step was to admit her to hospital where she could be observed and assessed and the right medication could be prescribed. At the time I was in the process of obtaining a Power of Attorney for Stella's care and I really didn't want her to be admitted to the dementia hospital. But it seemed to be the only way forward so that she could eventually come back to stay at home.

"The next day was the hardest day of my life. Dear Stella did not understand what was happening. We got into the car that morning. She did not know where we were going. As we were driving along Mumbles Road it was a beautiful clear morning and I remember looking up at the sky and seeing two crosses made by the vapour trails of two planes. I cried inwardly, somehow sensing that they were our crosses. I just had the feeling that our life together at home had come to an end.

"The hospital building was old - it was due to be pulled down in a couple of years' time. Stella was admitted to a mixed ward where visitors were not allowed in. There was a separate visitors' room where you could visit the patients. But because Stella could not settle without me being there, they allowed me to go into the ward. There were about twelve patients and a number of staff. Seeing the other patients and their behaviour was very distressing although I understood that they did not realise what they were doing. I felt for them and for the staff who worked there.

"When I had to leave Stella, which was so difficult, the staff had to let me out of the ward. The double doors to the ward were locked and they had two round glass windows in them. They drew Stella's attention away from me while I went out. Part of the way down the corridor, I heard Stella crying out aloud, 'Brian, Brian, help me, please help me' and a banging on the window. I turned and saw her face against the window. I just cried and cried. I wanted to turn back and bring her out. But I couldn't because I did not have the Power of Attorney to do this. So there was nothing I could do but to turn around and walk out crying and feeling so defeated that all I could do was say, 'Why, Father God.' That sight tormented me for months, seeing Stella at the door and hearing her voice crying out.

"In fact it continued to torment me from time to time until years later. Then one night I woke up at about 3.00a.m. It was the Tuesday before Easter. Again that memory of that time when I had to leave Stella in the dementia ward came flooding back. Again, I wept at the memory as I vividly recalled her face at the window as I had to turn my back and walk away from her. Suddenly Father God said to me, 'Now you know a LITTLE of how I felt when I had to turn My back on My only beloved Son. When He cried, *Why have You forsaken Me?* I cried too. I too had to put My only Son into a world of sin and allow the world to crucify Him as an offering for the sins of the world. I too had to watch and cry.'

"It made me realise afresh what it cost Father God to redeem the world and make all things new - it was by the giving of His only Son. This truly was God's love - a love demonstrated by the giving of His most precious gift to a world which was lost in sin and rebellion. 'God, who spared not His own Son, but delivered Him up for us all...' (Romans 8:32)

"This also reminded me of a prophetic word given by a well-known singer, Wintley Phipps, 'It is in the quiet crucible of your personal private suffering that your noblest dreams are born and God's greatest gifts are given in compensation of what you have been through.'

"For me that summed it all up, being put in the crucible of fire of suffering to allow Father God to bring out something so beautiful and meaningful.

"The Easter after I had that experience I shared it in a meeting. A pastor's wife later texted me and wrote. 'I just want to thank you for sharing this morning. The love of the Father in giving Jesus is so profound and I want to fully understand it just as you have through your experience with Stella.'

"Sometimes the only way that Father God can help us to understand His heart is to take us through a similar experience to make us see the cost of it all. We hear people say our salvation is free. And so it is. But it still cost Father God the greatest price He could ever pay. So never let us forget the price that had to be paid for our salvation.

Brian was now left at home all alone and thinking constantly about what was happening to Stella. He recalls, "Most times when I visited I had to go into the ward because they were afraid to let Stella out. This went on for 28 days and they were still not able to find the right medication.

"The doctor asked me if I would like Stella to be transferred into a new unit which was especially for women who had dementia. The unit had only been built six months before and there were three wards. They asked if I would like to go and look at the room that was vacant and reassured me that they could continue with finding out what the best medication should be. I was so glad to know that I could get Stella out of the old ward, so I went over to see the room.

"It was a large single room with an en-suite bathroom and the room opened onto a wide corridor which led to a lovely garden. It was a very modern ward and had all the high-tech equipment and facilities needed for people suffering with dementia. I agreed to the move and so we brought Stella over and settled her into the new single room. This made things much better for both of us. The visiting hours were from 2.00 to 4.00 in the afternoon and 6.00 to 8.00 in the evening. Once she had settled, they allowed me to take Stella out of the hospital at 2.00 in the afternoon and bring her back at 8.00 in the evening. This was a great arrangement and it meant I could take her home and make her dinner.

"She loved to go out in the car for a drive to Swansea Marina and sometimes down to Gower. Then we would often walk around for an hour or two and go and have a coffee and cake. Stella loved to sing as we walked and although I wasn't very good at it I was determined to give it a good try. From that time on we sang and walked around the marina, singing hymns aloud. We used to say that this was our time of evangelism. It was amazing how many people stopped us and asked us about the songs we were singing. Some would say,

'God bless you.' Our favourite song was *To God be the glory, great things He has done.* I knew that people could tell that Stella had dementia and yet everyone was so kind. She often had to hold on to me even though she loved to walk and didn't want to stop! She could walk for hours and often because of her condition she'd walk around the corridors of the ward, even in the night.

"One day I recall in particular. As we walked along the promenade we met a young eastern man, very nicely dressed and probably in his 30s. He walked past us very quickly then stopped suddenly and turned around to face us. We also stopped in surprise. He said, 'You are a beautiful couple,' lifted up his hand and said very sincerely, 'God bless you.' That really brought tears to our eyes. He then turned back around and went on his way down a side street. When we looked to see where he had gone he wasn't to be seen anywhere. It was like seeing an angel in disguise. We felt it was encouragement from the Lord to us. After our walks around the marina we always went into the café in the Waterfront Museum and the people who served us there were always so kind to us.

"Many times I took Stella to our flat in Mumbles but I'm sorry to say she never saw it as her home again because of the dementia. This was another step down. It was almost as though we were back in our courting days. Stella used to ask me where my mother was and whether it was alright for her to be here alone with me in the flat. This was the way it went with dementia, I just had to play along with it and make the best of the time we had together. It was like your whole life together going in reverse, just losing it little by little and seeing Stella age very quickly. Yet the love we had for each other grew even more deeply and continued to do so until the end of her life.

"About this time the two remaining houses which had comprised the Bible College of Wales, Derwen Fawr and Sketty Isaf, were put up for sale as housing development sites which made me feel very sad. We had spent such wonderful days there as students and workers and I had such precious memories of so many glorious spiritual experiences and blessings there. Then we heard the good news that a Singapore church called Cornerstone had purchased one of the properties. Pastor Yang, their senior pastor, came over and arranged to buy Derwen Fawr, the house and grounds with the College buildings. His vision was to once again to re-establish it as a college and a place of prayer and intercession. This is what we longed to see come into being.

"I offered to help when it was possible. They asked me if I would mind taking people around the grounds and telling them something of the history of the College. I was happy to do that and enjoyed meeting the many visitors who came. Later a church also began on the site which was named Liberty Church. I joined the family church with Stella which was a blessing. The church were very kind to us and Pastor Mark Ritchie's wife Mary and a church worker Jackie stepped in to give me a free day to rest by visiting Stella.

"I tried to go and take Stella out most days of the week. On some days we had to stay on the ward - always walking - sometimes just around the corridors of the ward. She just loved singing even on the ward. When I arrived Stella would always greet me by name and with a loving kiss. I only recall one terrible day when she did not know who I was. On that day I took her out in the car. She was willing to go and as we drove off I kept reassuring her by repeating that I was Brian her husband, but she couldn't understand and wouldn't believe me. She was obviously distressed and after an hour in the car I just had to take her back to the hospital.

"After I had taken her in, I got back into the car and cried. I pleaded with the Lord. 'Please, please Lord; do not take me down this road. I cannot take it.' I feared that this was going to be the next step down. However, in spite of my fears, when I went to see Stella on the following day, as I walked in, to my delight she said, 'Brian,' and gave me a big kiss. l was overjoyed. From that day onwards, Stella never forgot who l was. How I thank the Lord for His goodness to us and for answering prayer. He knows us so well and will not try us beyond our capacities.

"On one occasion while Stella was in hospital I was in a church meeting and enjoying a wonderful time of worship. Then Pastor Mark Ritchie did something unusual. He brought out a box and asked that if anyone had a need, whether it was for healing, financial or anything else, they should write it down on a piece of paper and place it into the box as an act of faith, giving the need over to the Lord. At that time I was thinking of dear Stella. I wrote her name down on the paper that I had and placed the paper into the box, symbolically giving her to the Lord and trusting Him to have His way in her life. As Pastor Mark prayed over the box, I fell to my knees weeping. Then the Lord then said to me, 'Now give into the collection according to the amount to which you love her.' When the offering box came all I had was forty pounds, so I put all that I had into the box - four times more than my usual gift.

"At the end of the service Pastor Mark came to me and asked, 'Brian, could you do something for me? I have eleven Australians wanting a tour around the grounds and the house. Could you help me by taking them around?' I said, 'I'm sorry Mark but I'm going to visit Stella.' But as soon as I'd said it the Lord challenged me and said, 'Have you not just given her to Me?' I responded immediately by asking the Lord's forgiveness and told Pastor Mark that I would be glad to do what he'd asked. He took me over and introduced the pastor and the other ten Australians to me.

"We all walked out of the conference hall door to begin the tour. As we did so the leader, Pastor Noel, approached me and said, 'I would like to give you this.' I saw that it was a bundle of notes. I answered, 'No thank you. I am only too happy to take you around.' He then replied, 'God has told me to give it to you,, and insisted that I accept it. I could not refuse it since he was adamant that it was something Father God had specifically asked him to do. So I accepted the money, putting in my pocket. Then we continued with the tour.

Figure 114 The Australian visitors with Richard and Kristine Maton who faithfully served the Lord at the Bible College. Richard has also written two wonderful books documenting the history of the College during the directorship of Samuel Howells.

"We had such a great time together and especially in a prayer time in the Blue Room in Derwen Fawr house. 1 didn't leave the group until 9.00 that evening. When I got home I emptied my pockets before going to bed. I pulled out the bundle of notes and counted them and there was one hundred pounds in twenty pound notes. Father God said to me, 'I saw how much you loved Stella; you gave everything you had. Well this is how much I love her.' I had given four times my usual amount and Father God had given me back ten times that amount. On my knees I just wept and thanked Him. I knew how much I cared for her, but He cared ten times more. That was so comforting to know. This was not about money - I gave it to the College.

Figure 115 Stella with Brian on a day out.

"The weeks went by and people in the church were so good in standing in for me when I needed time to myself and I had one day a week to rest. They wanted to give me more time but I wanted to spend as much time with Stella as I could, knowing she wanted me there all the time.

"But then, in June 2014, Stella began to have difficulty eating and started to choke on her food. She was given medication for this but two weeks later she had a severe bout of choking and now could not drink without choking. The following day the doctor and charge nurse called me into the office to have a talk. They were obviously concerned about Stella's deteriorating condition and wanted to discuss the options. I knew Stella did not want any intravenous feeding. She had shared with me her desire to go home and be with her Lord and Saviour. The doctor and charge nurse were very understanding, and respected our decision. It was then they decided to put her on palliative care to keep her comfortable and free from pain. They told me that I could come to visit at any time day or night as Stella was in the last stage of her life. They also told me that if I needed to stay, they had a room available so that I could sleep there.

"For the first three days I was there from early in the morning till late in the evening. I then went home to sleep and the staff said they would ring me if there was any change. On the third night at 1.00 in the morning they rang to say that Stella's breathing was shallow. I rushed in to be with her knowing the night nurses could not be with her all the time because she was in a single room and they had other patients in their care. I wanted to be there with her when Father God took her home to glory. They brought in a recliner chair and put it at the right side of the bed. This meant, 1 could lie down, put my hand under the bed sheets and hold on to her hand.

"Her breathing seemed to be normal. She was lying down with her eyes partly open but could not talk. The nurses came every two hours to turn her over. Her lips were very dry so I wet a corner of a cloth and helped her to suck it to moisten her lips. Then the nurses came and sorted out her oral needs and from then on her mouth looked much better.

"I had been there awake in the room on and off for 36 hours when, on the fifth night, holding onto Stella's hand under the sheets, I must have fallen asleep. I awoke on Friday at six o'clock in the morning. Stella was sitting up, eyes wide open, still not able to speak, but looking at me. I was taken aback. I thought, 'Lord what have you done?' I jumped off the chair, got down on my knees and told her how much I loved her and that Jesus would soon be coming to take her home. I began to tell her what heaven was like. I read scripture to her and prayed. This went on for 20 or 30 minutes. Then her eyes closed and she lay back down looking restful.

"The nurse came in with some breakfast for me. Later on that day Jackie, my good friend and church worker, came along to stay with Stella so that I could go and have a rest in the visitors' room. She promised to wake me if there was any change but after an hour or two I went back and took over once again. The doctor came at 4.15pm. I asked her how long she thought that Stella had. She thought it would be around 36 hours at the most. She left at 4.30pm and the nurses came in to turn Stella over. I was outside the room while they did this. I'd been outside for ten minutes and the nurses came out and said that her breathing had changed and asked me if I would like to go back in? I said, 'Yes' and I went in.

"I saw that Stella looked comfortable. I got down on my knees and looked at her. She appeared to be breathing as normal. I then started to pray and after a little while I prayed, 'Father God, I commit Stella into Your loving hands.' Looking once more at Stella, I again saw that her breathing seemed normal. Still holding onto her hand, I prayed again, and then Father God said to me, 'I want you to blow on her face.' I began to question what He asked and was not inclined to do it. But then the Lord spoke to me with a scripture, 'And God breathed into Adam and he became a living soul.' When I heard this I believed and realised that this truly was the Lord speaking to me.

"Holding on to Stella's hand, I put my head down again and prayed, 'Lord Jesus, I commit Stella's eternal spirit into your eternal arms.' Her breathing was just as normal as far as I could see and then I gently blew into her face, and immediately she stopped breathing! I was just stunned. I felt the presence of the Holy Spirit in the room. He gently took the eternal spirit of Stella out of her body. I had to let go of her hand and raised my hands in the air and just worshipped Him as I felt Him leave the room.

"There was such a sense of peace flooding the room and the presence of the Lord Jesus was so real. I could not help but rejoice just knowing that my beloved Stella was home with her Lord. I lowered my hands, looked at her, and all I saw was a shell. It was just so beautiful. I knew she was not there but was with the Lord Jesus. I went out to tell the nurses. They came and said they would have to get a doctor to certify the death.

"The two nurses came in to stay with me, while we waited for the doctor to come. They wanted to know how I met with Jesus. I shared my testimony and they wept. I told them that in a few days' time we would be committing this 'shell' of Stella into the ground, but that the Lord wanted them to know that one day the Lord Jesus was coming back to this world, not for this 'shell' but with Stella in a new resurrected body. They were filling up with tears. I felt so uplifted and had such peace knowing that she was with her Lord in her new beautiful home. It brought my own earlier experience back to me - of how lovely it is there, and again it awoke in me the longing to go home! After the doctor certified Stella's death, I left with Jackie and she kindly stayed with me to see that I was all right. We went and had a good meal because I had not eaten much for the past three days. I was so full of the peace of the Lord.

"But now I had to plan Stella's funeral all on my own which wasn't easy. After all the days I had spent in the hospital and the lack of sleep, my energy seemed to drain away and I became very tired. The date for the funeral was set for Monday, 30th June, 2014, the day after what would have been Stella's 76th birthday. On her birthday I went to the Chapel of Rest and placed a birthday card in the coffin, kissed her and said goodbye to my love knowing that we will meet again in the Lord's presence in glory.

"Liberty Church was very supportive to me and helped wherever they could in preparing the conference hall at the Bible College for the funeral and providing refreshments. I was so thankful that my family were able to come and be with me. It made things a lot easier. When the day of the funeral came I was also glad to see a number of people there from the CLC mission with whom we had served together. There was a good attendance and it was a wonderful time of celebration, not of mourning.

"It was fitting that through the kindness and generosity of the church, the funeral service was held in the conference hall at the Bible College of Wales. It was here in that very hall that Stella and I had dedicated our lives to Father God and where the Lord baptised Stella in the Holy Spirit and now it was here where we committed her to the Lord. It was truly a time of celebration. As we were taking the coffin out of the conference hall, the whole congregation stood and clapped her out, praising Him for her life and the wonderful things that she had achieved for her Lord and Saviour Jesus Christ."

18. The Redemption of Derwen Fawr

In the months after Stella's home call it felt as though my life had come to a sudden halt. From the situation where I'd had so much to do, suddenly everything seemed to stop. I began to throw myself into helping, in any way I could with the Bible College.

I have already mentioned how sad I had been to hear that the Bible College had been put up for sale late in 2010, but how pleased I was to hear about a visit to Wales in 2011 by the Cornerstone Community Church, Singapore led by their senior pastor, Pastor Yang. During that visit and following his return to Singapore he had been prompted to redeem Derwen Fawr with the object of re-establishing the Bible College of Wales for the blessing and benefit of Wales and the nations.

I first had contact with Pastor Yang when I was invited by a friend to go to a meeting following the completion of Cornerstone's purchase of Derwen Fawr. Pastor Yang shared how much the book *Rees Howells Intercessor* had influenced and spoken into his life, as well as the history of the 1904 Welsh Revival. He went on to say that the Bible College of Wales had been bought as a thank-you offering to Wales for what missionaries, saved in the Welsh Revival, did in bringing the gospel to Singapore and also what Great Britain did for Singapore in the Second World War. His vision and desire was to see the Bible College restored and once again functioning as a college to the glory of God and the blessing of the nations.

As the meeting went into a time of prayer, the Lord spoke to me and prompted me to share a prophetic word with Pastor Yang. The Lord said, "The first thing you must do is to replace the memorial stone to its original spot in front of the house, for there would be no blessing without it being put back in its rightful place." In fear and trembling I went up to Pastor Yang as he was praying, I put my arms around him and gave him the Lord's word.

I have already described this stone. At the dedication of Derwen Fawr in 1931 and as a testament and a witness to God's faithfulness and providence, Rees Howells had removed a statue which stood on a stone plinth at the front of the house and replaced it with a simple oval stone which had written on one side "Jehovah Jireh" and on the other side "Faith is Substance". However, this had been moved in recent years to unify the front lawn and make more room for recreation, and it had been repositioned against the back of the bake-house building. As it was being moved with a forklift truck, the top of the stone which had the writing on broke in two pieces. The marble insets on which the words were inscribed had broken and had been replaced with a new marble oval inscribed with the original words.

Figure 116 Brian at the plinth in front of Derwen Fawr House

After Cornerstone completed the purchase of the site in late 2012, the work then began to bring the Bible College of Wales back to life and Pastor Yang saw to it that the plinth was now moved back to its original position in front of the house.

Pastor Mark Ritchie was the man Pastor Yang put in charge to oversee the project. While work commenced on the restoration of the College buildings, Mark invited people from various churches to join him in prayer for the College and revival every Tuesday morning. These Tuesdays became a real time of blessing for people who were drawn from all over Wales and also attracted visitors from all over the world. Out of this a church was established in 2013 which became known as Liberty Church. It was there that Stella and I became part of the church family. The church began to grow quite quickly and was held in the conference hall of the Bible College. It was there in that hall where Stella and I gave everything to the Lord in 1964. It was also where Stella was baptised in the Holy Spirit and then where on June 30th, 2014 we celebrated Stella's home call to glory. By mid-2014 the work there was progressing quickly and the inauguration of the College was planned for May 2015.

Figure 117 The conference hall today

During those days many groups came to visit the Bible College of Wales from all over the world. Many ex-students and staff came to visit. Many others came because they had read Norman Grubb's book, *Rees Howells, Intercessor*, and because they had heard that the Bible College was to be restored. Many simply wanted to spend time praying in the College grounds. The two phrases that most of the groups used were "reclaiming our inheritance" (of prayer and intercession) and "opening up the wells" (praying for revival).

Because of my seven years' experience at the Bible College and knowing its history, I was often asked if I would take visitors around. This became such a blessing to me and a ministry which I am happy to say is still continuing to this day.

There was one particular experience that I would like to share. It occurred two or three weeks before the re-opening of the Bible College. I was being interviewed in Derwen Fawr house and as they finished they asked me if they could take some photos of me by the well. As far as I knew the old well was covered over with weeds and wild thorn bushes and that there was nothing to see. They still wanted to go down to the well, so I agreed and as we approached it I was amazed to see that all the weeds and the thorn bushes had been cleared away.

I went to sit on the stone at the side of the well while they were taking photos, and as I sat there the Lord said to me, "Open your Bible to Revelation 21:1-7." On doing so and reading it, the Spirit of Father God just came on me; then I just began to weep and weep; I could not stop. The passage is a wonderful vision given to John of a restored heaven and earth - God's fulfilment of His promise to dwell among His people in everlasting peace and joy, and His gift of the fountain of the water of life freely to all who thirst. My mind went back to the time when Duncan Campbell spoke and God's glory came down in the prayer room.

Figure 118 Brian at the well, now reopened and cleared

Figure 119 Brian at the well

I felt like Simeon when Mary and Joseph brought baby Jesus to him. He said, "Lord, now You are letting Your servant depart in peace, according to Your word; for my eyes have seen Your salvation." With tears in my eyes, I felt like him, as though in some way my work had finished and I was content to go home to glory. I was so overjoyed.

18. The Redemption of Derwen Fawr

That happened on a Thursday, and on the Friday I went to our weekend church conference which was being held in mid-Wales where the speaker was John Andrews. On the Friday night his message was on "Seeing the Vision". When he had finished and as I stood up to leave, the wife of one of our elders, Pam, came up to me crying and sobbing. She put her arms around me and said through her tears, "Brian, the Lord has told me to tell you that you are like Simeon and that I am not going to take you home until you have really, really seen My glory." I was completely taken aback because she knew nothing of what had taken place at the well. I had thought that the Lord was preparing me for my departure to be with Him and that had filled me with joy, but now it seemed that He had another purpose in mind.

I feel very privileged to receive such a word from Father God. I firmly believe that there is a great move of God coming through a true revival where we are going to see men and women falling down under the power of the Holy Spirit in true repentance and finding salvation through Christ Jesus our Lord. To think I'm going to have the privilege of seeing the beginning of it is overwhelming. Wow!

A month or two before, a group of volunteers from Liberty Church began to restore the gardens of the Bible College. We were all asked if we would like to contribute some flowers or shrubs for the garden. I went to a garden centre to get some roses and while there I saw a beautiful magnolia tree full of flowers. On looking at the label, I was surprised to see it was called *Stellata*, like Stella, which means star. I thought it was a lovely tree to plant in memory of Stella. I purchased it, took it to the College and we planted it in the College garden; it was in full flower and looked beautiful.

A few weeks later, all the flowers had gone and then all the leaves began to drop off, as though the tree was dying. I went back to the garden centre. They told me to feed it with a fertiliser they gave me. Yet after a few weeks it was still dying. I asked a friend who was a keen gardener to look at it. She could tell that there seemed to be no sap in it and it was dead. I left it for another week. Then the Lord said to me, "Pull it up," so I did. The roots were dry; I broke it up and threw it into the bin. Then I asked the Lord. "Why did that have to happen?"

Figure 120 Stella's Grave

I went to the car and drove off with tears in my eyes. Not knowing where to go, I went up to the graveside, had a cry and said, "Sorry love." I then drove home feeling really sad. When I got there I found an envelope in the post and when I opened it I found that it contained a new worship CD by Tom Read. I didn't have a clue who had sent it to me. I began to listen to it immediately, and to my amazement the song I heard was:

Do not stand at my grave and weep.
I am not there, I do not sleep.
Do not stand at my grave and cry
I am not there. I am alive.

I was so astonished at what I was hearing! The next song was:

The Spirit of the Sovereign Lord
Is on me now
To love, to speak, to heal, to preach
The Spirit of the Sovereign Lord
Is on me now, giving life.

You turn ashes to beauty
Mourning to dancing
Anguish to songs of praise.

Pour Your Spirit over me
Let Your love rain down
Would You take these hands of mine
And use me
Pour Your Spirit over me
Let Your love rain down
Would You take these feet of mine
And lead me.

How the Good Lord spoke to me through those words! What more could have been said. I was so amazed and blessed! All I could do was to dance before Him and give Him all the praise and glory - just through that assurance of knowing that Stella is alive and now with her Lord and Saviour Jesus Christ and that He was calling me to tell of the wonderful things He has done; to give myself afresh to Him so that He might fulfil His will and purpose in my life.

In May 2015, the Bible College of Wales was dedicated and inaugurated. What a day of fulfilment and blessing it was. Many distinguished guests came to the inauguration and there followed a weekend of wonderful ministry with Lou Engels and Dutch Sheets from the USA. It was the crowning day of so much prayer and also so much selfless generosity on the part of the leadership and congregation of Cornerstone Community Church, Singapore. That week I had the honour and privilege of being asked by Pastor Yang to serve as an adviser at the College, which I was happy to accept.

Since that day (written in mid-2016) two successful leadership courses have been run at the College and the students who have attended from all over the world have contributed to the ongoing prayer and intercession that continues to be at the heart of the College. The students are such a blessing in so many ways. They have gone out into the world equipped for service and with hearts set ablaze with God's love. Regular intercession continues at the College for the nations, especially those where Christians are persecuted and are suffering for their faith. The word of God, quoted by our Lord, is still the watchword, "My house shall be a place of prayer for all nations."

There is a special place at the College for intercession for this land of Wales - a land which the Lord has been pleased to visit so many times in revival blessing and from which so many people have gone out to the nations to take the glorious gospel of Jesus Christ to those who have not heard. The College through the staff and students, in the days of Rees Howells and his son and successor Samuel, has not only sent many men and women out into the world to fulfil our Lord's commission to "Go into all the world and proclaim the gospel to every creature", but also through intercession and prayer provided the support both spiritual and practical to those who went. That work continues in these days. Cornerstone Church, under the leadership of Pastor Yang Tuck Yoong, has a world-wide vision for mission, and Wales and the nations are blessed by the selfless giving that has made the redemption of the Bible College of Wales possible.

The work to restore the other buildings at the College continues. The bake-house block has been converted to student accommodation as has the men's hostel, which means that all of the students can be accommodated on site from early 2017. Liberty Church has been entrusted with the wonderful Siloh chapel in the Brynhyfryd district of Swansea, and work on the chapel will commence shortly. Pisgah chapel, where Evan Roberts first ministered to the young people of Moriah chapel at Loughor at the commencement of the 1904 Welsh Revival, has been restored by Cornerstone and is in use as a prayer centre.

As I continue to serve the Lord since my dear Stella went home, I feel that my main role centres around the College, firstly in continuing the intercession and also in being available to visitors and ex-students of the College who come in increasing numbers since the Visitor Centre is open in Derwen Fawr house.

The intercession ministry has a number of focuses in the two years we have been meeting. First of all, as I have said, there is a burden for the persecuted church worldwide. We live in a day where our Christian brothers and sisters are under an enormous amount of pressure all over the world. Many live under repressive regimes and are subject to imprisonment, abuse, torture and execution. Many more live in constant danger in the many war-torn areas of the world.

Then there is the situation here in Swansea, in Wales and in the United Kingdom. The condition of the Christian church here in Wales gives great cause for concern. Many once thriving chapels and churches are either at the point of closing or are closed. As a nation, the UK has made a decision to leave the European Union and its secular leadership, and our nation and government need not only prayer support in order to set our future direction but also the nation is in need of godly men and women to be in positions of authority.

But most encouragingly, it appears that the Lord is raising up intercessors from all over the world with a burden that God would again visit His people with a mighty revival which would spread like fire through the nations and result in a mighty harvest of souls in these end days of time before our Lord's glorious return. That is the answer to all of the problems that confront us and the wider world. As Isaiah prayed, "Oh, that You would rend the heavens! That You would come down! That the mountains might shake at Your presence - As fire burns brushwood, As fire causes water to boil - To make Your name known to Your adversaries, that the nations may tremble at Your presence!" Isaiah 64:1-2.

19. Reflection - Past and Future

I would just like to share with you how Father God is leading me forward, and also what I feel that His purpose is for my life at this time. As I have reflected on my life, my mind goes back to my first year at the Bible College.

I often wondered why Father God took me on my own to College for the first year. In July 1964 Father God had spoken to us both very clearly in several ways and we both understood that we were called to sell up all that we had and take up our cross and follow Him. We also understood clearly that the first step was to go to Bible College, but when we applied to Glasgow College and were turned down we were a bit taken aback and wondered why. God's call on our lives was confirmed at the Bible College of Wales' "Every Creature" conference when Duncan Campbell spoke of laying everything on the altar. It was from that point that we committed ourselves and never looked back.

And yet when I returned to Blackburn at the end of the conference, Stella knew from the Lord not only that it was not her time to go to College but also that it was my time, and she lovingly released me to the Lord to go to the Bible College of Wales.

When I reflect again on that first year, I realise afresh that the one incident that stood out above all others was the visit of Rev. Duncan Campbell to speak over a weekend. At the end of his stay, at the Monday morning service the glory of God came down in the Prayer Room at Derwen Fawr House. This experience was so powerful and glorious that it left a longing in my heart to see such a move of God in a fresh revival of His church. That longing has not diminished over the years

On another visit later in that first year, Duncan Campbell asked Mr. Samuel if he could meet with me. When I went to him in the Green Room at Derwen Fawr he asked me to share my testimony and then spent some time praying over me. However, that meeting left some unanswered questions and I didn't really understand what had prompted it and what its purpose was, although I asked the Lord about it.

In 1971/72, Duncan Campbell visited the College for the last time before he died. I was privileged to hear him give his final account of the revival in the Hebrides. From 1965 to 2015 (50 years) I have been blessed with many wonderful hours in fellowship with the Lord, but in all those years I have never experienced anything like the presence of God on that Monday morning in 1965. Why did Duncan Campbell single me out for prayer? Did God show him some reason for it? Was he in some way passing the baton on to me?

In May 2015, just before the College inauguration, I had the powerful experience at the newly-discovered well in the College grounds (described in the previous chapter). At first, my overwhelming reaction was that like Simeon I was ready to go home and be with Stella in that wonderful heavenly realm that I had experienced when I had my stroke. But the prophetic word I received the following night made it clear that the Lord was not going to take me home until I had "really, really seen His glory"(the exact words). This word was so strong and it made a deep impression on me.

As I've meditated on these things, I believe I see the providential will of Father God at work over my life. In 1964 Father God had to take me away on my own for that year. At the time it was a break in our marriage, but at the end of the year he made it possible for Stella and me to be together again and to follow Him and fulfil all His purposes for our lives together until the day of Stella's home call.

But then I recall one final significant incident. Just as Stella had lovingly released me at the beginning of our marriage, so also, just a few weeks before her home call, she said to me, "Brian, I want to release you to fulfil what the Lord has for you to do with whosoever Father God will bring alongside you to complete His commission."

I don't know what Father God has in store for the future, but the One who called Stella and me to follow Him and to trust Him with our lives has promised to lead me and guide me and be with me. My eyes remain firmly on Him.

Postscript: Why I Wrote This Book

One day while I was walking in the park, I met a Christian friend who is a retired judge. I had not seen him for quite a while. He asked about Stella. I told him her story and what had happened to her. He then said to me, "You've got to write a book."

I met a young man from Singapore at the Bible College, who was over in Wales with his in-laws. He invited me to have breakfast with them and he asked me to share my story. When I told them what the Lord had taken me through, his father-in-law, who also happened to be a retired judge, said, "You've got to write a book."

After hearing this from two retired judges, I then began asking the Lord, "Is this really what You want me to do - to write a book? Give me a hammer and nails and then I'm a happy man, but give me a pen and paper, and I am completely outside of my comfort zone." I said, "It's not in me, Lord."

But as always the Lord knew what He was doing. It was then he sent a brother who came alongside me, a Welshman called Dave Jones, to help me get it all down on paper. It took much time and hard work, but it was very rewarding. We spent time together in conversation and I spent time filling in the gaps by writing them up on my iPad and emailing what I had written to him.

On 7th April, 2016, at 2.00 in the morning I had finished writing on Stella and our lives together. I felt so relieved to have finished it. At the end of that day I went to a meeting in the evening to hear one of the visiting lecturers speak at a public meeting at the Bible College. The speaker was Steve Carpenter who is serving the Lord and living in Israel. I went to have a talk with him after the meeting and mentioned that I was a student at the College in the 60s. He bowed his head in deep thought and then asked, "What's your name?" After telling him, he then said, "I see the cover of a book and at the bottom is your name, Brian Halliwell." Then he said, "You've got to write your story." I was astonished and answered, "I just finished the book at two o'clock this morning!" He then asked, "What's the title?" I told him, "Tell them that I am alive". He said, "I want to read it."

Shortly after this, I met up with another friend, also called Dave. He also said to me that I needed to finish the book with a last section to bring my story up to the present day. And so it is that I have added these final two chapters to let all who will read this know that the Lord still continues to speak to me and use me in prayer and intercession and prophetic ministry, and above all to fulfil His commission to me to witness that He is alive.

I trust the Lord will bless you through this book. I pray that also you will know Him - our Lord and Saviour Jesus Christ, and that Father God, through His Holy Spirit, may lead you into prayer and intercession. Paul tells us that we are seated in the heavenly places in Christ Jesus and He is our Great Intercessor. Our commission is to bring heaven down to earth, in accordance with the will of our Father God.

We must never forget that while we are here, we are on a battlefield and in the midst of a great battle against a powerful enemy. But he is a defeated foe. The battle was won at Calvary upon a cruel cross. Ultimately, planet earth has nothing to compare with heaven's glory. Be blessed, heaven is real; I've been there. Finally, I will tell you again what Jesus told me to tell you, His message to you is simple and life changing - "I AM ALIVE."

Yours in our Lord Jesus Christ, Brian Halliwell.

Some Further Resources

Updates and News It is hoped that these will be published in due course including a selection of colour photographs from the book at www.brianhalliwell.com Brian can be contacted via email at brian@brianhalliwell.com

CLC International. For news and information about the ongoing ministry of CLC visit http://clc.org.uk

Rees Howells, Intercessor by **Norman Grubb**. Originally published by the Lutterworth Press, it is currently available in a number of reprinted editions, one of which is by Cornerstone Resources Pte Ltd of Singapore. This is essential reading for those who want to understand how the original Bible College of Wales was founded and the remarkable life of Rees Howells, a man of great faith and vision.

Samuel, Son and Successor of Rees Howells, Director of the Bible College of Wales – A Biography by **Richard A. Maton**. Published in June 2012 by ByFaith Media. Richard Maton served at the Bible College from 1956 and served as a teacher, lecturer, dean, trustee and principal. He is married to Kristine who also has been associated with the College since 1936. This book tells the story of the College during the years from 1950 to 2004 and beyond in great detail.

Samuel Rees Howells, a Life of Intercession, the Legacy of Prayer and Spiritual Warfare of an Intercessor by **Richard A. Maton**. Published by ByFaith Media November 2012. Richard Maton's second book gives a detailed account of the prayer and intercession of Samuel Howells who followed in his father Rees's footsteps. Essential reading for those who are passionate about interceding for the furtherance of God's kingdom in this world.

The Intercession of Rees Howells by **Doris M. Ruscoe and Norman Grubb.** Published by the Lutterworth Press. Doris M. Ruscoe joined the College staff in 1932 and became headmistress of Emmanuel Grammar School at the College. The book provides many insights regarding College life and the prayer and intercession that continued among the College staff throughout the Second World War. It also contains valuable notes taken at the regular Bible readings at the College given by Rees Howells which give a rich insight into his thinking and prayer.

Miss Doris Ruscoe – Principles of Intercession. In the year that Emmanuel Grammar School celebrated its jubilee and Miss Ruscoe celebrated her 80th birthday, the former headmistress gave a recorded interview which is available online at http://christasus.podbean.com/e/doris-ruscoe-principle-of-intercession/. Miss Ruscoe was present at the College throughout the Second World War and witnessed and took part in the intercession at the College. An amazing testimony from a lady who knew Rees Howells personally, and the interview gives the listener an invaluable insight into the principles of intercession.

David Pike (Welldigger) has blogged extensively on all aspects of Welsh Christian history, particularly with regard to revival history. He has a series of blogs on Rees Howells and the Bible College of Wales, the Revival in Gazaland and Rees Howells' involvement. More recently he has also told the story behind The Redemption of Derwen Fawr, which includes details of its purchase and restoration led by Pastor Yang Tuck Yoong and Cornerstone Community Church of Singapore. David's blog can be found at http://daibach-welldigger.blogspot.co.uk.

The official BCW website has brilliant photographs and lots of information about the College, the background to its redemption and current courses - http://www.bcwales.org/.

BCW is on Facebook at Bible College of Wales where day-to-day information on current activities and some excellent photographs are to be found

Cornerstone Community Church

Website at http://www.cscc.org.sg/ contains resources and an introduction to the pastor and church that were obedient to the vision of redeeming the Bible College of Wales as a strategic resource for the Kingdom of God in this generation. Their love and passion and commitment to Wales are truly amazing.

David Davies. You can still find a fascinating talk given by David Davies at BCW on the subject of Congo Revival of 1953/54 online and it is still possible to find texts online of David Davies' account of the Simba rebellion. *With God in Congo Forests* and *The Captivity and Triumph of Winnie Davies*, both originally published by WEC.

Intercession for Revival. There are a number of websites which provide encouragement and information regarding prayer and intercession for revival. Dick and Gladys Funnell have been praying in Wales for many years and host a website at http://www.walesawakening.org/

http://www.moriahchapel.org.uk/ is the website of Moriah chapel, the birthplace of the 1904 Revival at Loughor.

http://www.pisgahchapel.com/ is the website of the redeemed and restored Pisgah Chapel, a schoolroom where Evan Roberts began his ministry in 1904. Again the restoration was carried out by the Cornerstone Community Church under the leadership of Pastors Tuck Yoong and Daphne Yang.

Photographs

Photographs

Endnotes

[1] Rodney "Gypsy" Smith, MBE (1860-1946) was a British evangelist who conducted evangelistic campaigns in the UK and USA for over 70 years. He was born to Romany parents in a tent on Epping Forest. He taught himself to read and write and was an early member of the Salvation Army. He travelled extensively and drew crowds of thousands.

[2] Edwin F. Harvey and his wife Lillian were an American couple who spent many years in the UK. Edwin was a principal of a Bible school in Glasgow before launching MOVE in 1956 - an interdenominational evangelistic movement. Edwin was a man of prayer and of the Word and may be best known for *Kneeling we triumph*, two volumes of daily readings on prayer which are still available.

[3] Rowland and Ann later became the founders of World Horizons, an organisation which provides opportunities for young people who are committed to evangelism going on short or long-term mission at home and abroad. See http://worldhorizons.co.uk

[4] In 1964 the Bible College of Wales consisted of the three early estates that the Lord had led Rees Howells to buy. Glynderwen (Oak Valley) which was the home of Emmanuel School and Derwen Fawr (Great Oak) and Sketty Isaf (Lower Sketty), both of which were used by the Bible College.

[5] On Boxing Day morning in 1934, Rees Howells received the commission from the Lord to pray that in the following 30 years the Lord would provide for the sending and maintenance of missionaries to fulfil our Lord's commission to "Go into all the world and preach the gospel to every creature." See *Rees Howells Intercessor*, Chapter 30. The commission was taken up and carried on through Rees's son Samuel - see Richard Maton's *Samuel, Son and Successor of Rees Howells*, Page 107. Also Richard Maton's *Samuel Rees Howells: A Life of Intercession*, chapter 13 and 20. In concrete terms this entailed praying in £100,000 pounds and also, more significantly, interceding strategically for the furtherance of the gospel in the face of much opposition..

[6] Duncan Campbell was a Scottish minister who was used greatly in the Hebridean Revival of 1949-53. He arrived on the Isle of Lewis for a 10-day mission at the request of a local minister and in answer to the prayers of two elderly and infirm ladies who had been assured that he would come. He was in much demand as a speaker and shared what God had done in the Hebrides. He also had a powerful preaching and teaching ministry.

[7] Derwen Fawr has two large rooms at the front of the building, the Green Room to the left of the entrance and the Blue Room to the right. Up to the Second World War the main meeting room was at the back left of the house, but during the

war intercession was carried on in the Blue Room. The rooms have been extensively and beautifully restored by Cornerstone Community Church, Singapore, and both the Blue and the Green Room form the main part of the Visitor Centre and Exhibition today.

[8] Writer's Note: While I was in the process of preparing this book, I met a lady whose father had been a Christian travelling salesman who was also a friend of the Bible College. He regularly visited Idwal and Gwladys Thomas at their shop in Dowlais and knowing that they were both Christians, he mentioned the Bible College to them. Sometime later they sold up the business and both offered themselves full-time to the Lord at BCW. In the 1950s Gwladys pioneered the school at Ramallah with others and Idwal became a baker at the College and also a trustee in Samuel's day. Richard Maton in his book *Samuel, Son and Successor to Rees Howells* tells how close Samuel and Idwal became, being able to converse in Welsh and also of the successful intercession that was made for Idwal when he was admitted with peritonitis and was close to death in the early 60s. See page 261 Ch 26.

[9] After the Chilean earthquake disaster of 2010, the decision was made to return the bells to Santiago for the 150th anniversary of the fire in 2013.

[x] Today Chile is nominally between 50 and 60 per cent Roman Catholic, but some 15 per cent of the population describe themselves as evangelical which applies to all Protestant groups. Among the evangelicals approximately 90 per cent are Pentecostal. The Pentecostal Church in Chile was unusually born out of the Methodist Church, hence the denomination is known as the Pentecostal Methodist Church. Jotabeche is the Pentecostal Cathedral of Chile and today seats 18,000 people. A modern assessment by "Chile for Christ" reckons that the numbers of Pentecostal worshippers in Chile may even exceed those who regularly attend Mass. For many years the Jotabeche church had the largest membership in the world - only more recently overtaken by churches in Korea. Its rapid growth has been attributed to its witness teams that preach on the streets of Santiago every Sunday. CLC was a major player in providing Christian Literature in Chile and a vital resource for growth of Christianity in the country.

45290717R00128

Printed in Poland
by Amazon Fulfillment
Poland Sp. z o.o., Wrocław